The Longest Goodbye:
A Memoir

Helena Farrell

as told-to-by Marcia Temple

authorHOUSE®

AuthorHouse™
1663 Liberty Drive
Bloomington, IN 47403
www.authorhouse.com
Phone: 1-800-839-8640

First published by AuthorHouse 10/2/2009

ISBN: 978-1-4490-3047-6 (e)
ISBN: 978-1-4490-3046-9 (sc)
ISBN: 978-1-4490-3045-2 (hc)

Printed in the United States of America
Bloomington, Indiana

This book is printed on acid-free paper.

This book is dedicated to the memory of my parents.
Marcia Temple

With gratitude and appreciation,
this book is dedicated to my husband,
Joseph T. Farrell, M.D.

Helena C. Farrell

Introduction

It is October 2004, and I'm sitting alone in my apartment in Florida searching for answers to my unanswered questions. Where have the years gone? As I reflect back upon my life, I recognize that my life's choices have determined where I am today. I ask myself, if I had my life to do over, what would I have done differently? What would I not have changed? What would I recommend and caution the young, presumably sophisticated people of today? This is a cautionary tale – a memoir of deep love, uncontrollable passion, untamed sex, devastating loss, betrayal, and painful awareness.

My bold and no doubt naïve intent for revealing this story is to keep other young women and men from heading into a similar destructive path of seduction by untamed passion because it clouds the mind, steals the heart, and distorts one's frame of moral guidance and reference. Love can be beautiful, everlasting, and endearing, but the need for awareness of the polar difference between perfect love and dangerous love is the moral of this tale. The search for this universal truth is centuries old, a journey that continues today. Let my journey begin.

Chapter One

RUNNING AWAY – TO WHERE?

Can one truly run away from their past? I thought I could by leaving New York City, a city with many faces, a city with many stories, a city with many secrets. It is October 2004, and I'm a 63-year-old divorced woman living alone in Florida. I've been divorced for over fifteen years and am still unaware about where my life is heading. I bravely put on a façade of contentedness, but I've made myself that way because I have no other options. I'm in my apartment watching reruns of the TV show *Sex and the City.* This extremely popular show jars my memory of a series of exciting and desperate events that took me away from my beloved Manhattan and the man I loved deeply. I thought that by going to Florida, the complete opposite of New York, I could run away from the haunting memories that started in the Big Apple. Sadly, though, the warmth and beauty of Florida could not erase my memories. The flow of the ocean, the softness of the sand, and the swaying palm trees could neither soothe nor heal my pain. My story of sex and the city began more than fifteen years ago – the centuries-old story of woman and man meeting and falling in love, a meditation of love's ebbs and flows. My story has many harrowing twists and turns. This is not the usual story of romance, love, and marriage but an introspect into my choices in life. This is how it all began; this is how my destiny unfolded.

The story begins when I was a married woman heading into my forties – an unsettling time in one's life. It was at this point that I met a seductively handsome man eight years my junior who permanently changed my life. Prior to our meeting, my life was a typical one. I was a young, attractive suburban, upper-middle-class Jewish girl growing up in the fifties. I had a good life. I was blessed with successful professional parents. I went to camp as a kid and had plenty of dates as a teenager. Since my parents belonged to a country club, I lived the typical country club lifestyle. As a young girl growing up in the fifties, I was expected to marry the right person. During that era, a young woman's goal was to meet a promising man, marry, buy a home, and have children. But that was not my goal. I always lived on the edge – I was always independent. Still, secretly, I always dreamed of having someone to take care of me. I was considered beautiful. I was very popular, and I was smart. Not intellectually. I considered myself streetwise more than anything else. Many young men pursued me, but, I also pursued. As smart as I thought I was, my judgment was marred. I was always attracted to and eventually married all the wrong men.

Looking back, I realize that I was drawn to men who represented excitement and glamour. I was in constant search of the thrill. I never looked for security or true love. My first marriage was very brief. Soon after we married, my first husband and I moved to Beverly Hills, California, into a beautiful home where we had an active, high-powered social life. After three unhappy years, we divorced because it was a loveless union. We married for all the wrong reasons. It was a childless marriage. Five years later, I met my second husband. He was a handsome man living in New York, and he was a challenge, which, of course, attracted me to him. It's the game of winning, conquering, being in control and on top that exhilarated me. I pursued him with a vengeance and won! We were together for over fifteen years, and it was a good marriage, at least as far as the outside world could see. He had a child from his previous marriage. We had money, the right house, the prestigious car, and socially prominent friends, yet these were not enough for me. I felt unfulfilled and empty; I felt unsettled in a way that could not be resolved. Our marriage lacked warmth. My needs were not being met, and because of that, I was not content. Something was missing in my life. I felt lonely even while my husband and dear friends surrounded me. At that time, I wasn't sure what was causing this emptiness. Later, for the first time in my life, I would find out what passionate, lust, and untamed love was all about. I recognize now that my marriage was void of mutual understanding, commitment, and unconditional love. Ironically, my husband and I never fought. We were good friends. On the surface, all seemed well.

Chapter Two

DISILLUSIONMENT AND SOLUTION?

It was 1980, and I was heading toward the dangerous forties. One day, after my routine physical, I was sitting in my gynecologist's private office crying. He asked me what was wrong and I blurted out, "I must be going through my middle-age crisis." My gynecologist denied me my feelings. He responded that I had everything a woman my age would want: a successful marriage, a good husband, plenty of money, and numerous friends. So, when my doctor said something in jest, I took it seriously. He said, "Go and have a fling. It will make you feel better." Affairs of the heart are so delicate that a vulnerable person, ripe for any answer, is susceptible to such benign, innocent suggestions. It actually crossed my mind to take his advice, but, I thought, with whom? In retrospect, the answer was stored in the deep subconscious of my mind.

As fate would have it, a couple of months later, my close friend Anna called me and asked me to meet her in New York City for lunch. She was going to a high-priced Madison Avenue jewelry salon to pick out a gift for her husband to give to her for her birthday. Anna, her husband, my former husband, and I had met years ago when we were on vacation. We clicked immediately; we all got along famously. Anna and I contrasted and complimented each other; she was a stunning, earthy, blond and I was dark auburn-haired and classy. There were many times when, unbeknownst to each of us, we dressed identically – like twins. She knew my inner-most secrets, and I knew hers. So it was not unusual for me to go into New York and pick out an expensive piece of jewelry with her. We strolled with confidence and gusto down Madison Avenue arm in arm and excited about her future purchase and our carefree time together. It was a gorgeous sunny spring day; my spirits were soaring. I experienced an unexpected fullness of heart. When we entered the jewelry store that day, my eyes immediately were drawn to this very strikingly dark-eyed, long and wavy black-haired, slightly built, sexy young man, 30ish, who was standing behind the jewelry showcase. His intense eyes pierced into mine, almost setting me off balance. At first I thought he was Israeli, but he was Middle Eastern. Later I found out his name was Kamil. As I gazed at him, his eyes stared back at me. As handsome as he was, if you took him apart, he was not physically perfect. He had small lips and a prominent nose, and was slim of hips, but putting the entire package together – his long, wild hair; his dark, piercing eyes; his sensual, confident walk; and the way he wore his clothes – he was sexy, and alluring. He always wore a flashy diamond pinky ring, and in the winter, a long raccoon fur coat. Kamil was a Mel Gibson type. He would stop any woman dead in her tracks. Love is blind, and I was intrigued by his flash and carefree confidence. Neither of us knew it at the moment, but this was the beginning of a long, dynamic, intensely sensual, dramatic, dangerously illicit, and sexually romantic relationship.

As the months passed, I couldn't stop thinking about this exotic, sexy man. Thoughts of him consumed me. I kept finding random reasons to go to the jewelry store. I went in there with various aimless reasons – to buy this, to talk to someone, whatever excuse to see him again. My gynecologist's words keep running around in my head. "Have a fling. It will do you good." Whenever I went in there, I noticed him looking at me seductively; he was definitely coming on to me. With a strong magnetic pull, I was drawn to him; he was my sexual fantasy. With all this magnetism, I still stayed aloof. I kept reminding myself that I was a married woman. The old-world rules about commitment, honor, and marital fidelity were ingrained in me as a child, and now those rules haunted me.

After some inquiring, I learned that he was also a married man with two young children. Early on, our flirtatious looks never amounted to anything, although he kept dropping little hints about going out for a drink. I kept saying "No." But I'm sure my lustful eyes communicated something different. I had always been a flirt, and I enjoyed it, so I continued to flirt with him. I wasn't sure what I wanted from him, but deep down, I did want him! I tried to rationalize the situation. I had a good life, a fine husband, and many devoted friends. I asked myself over and over again, "What are you doing?" I was forty and very attractive. I had a lot to offer. Everyone turned their heads when my husband and I walked into a room. I wasn't married to someone who was unattractive. My husband, David, was a slim, 6'2", green-eyed, salt and pepper-haired gorgeous man. He resembled the movie star Robert Wagner. But when it comes to the affairs of the heart, no one thinks rationally. The heart wants what it wants. Do we ever know what we are doing when our hearts are clouded over with desire? The intrigue, the mystery, and the fear of getting caught become seductive addictions.

After that first encounter, time went on uneventfully. The summer of 1980, my husband and I took a European trip. While there, I bought a strikingly beautiful outfit from Yves Saint-Laurent. I will never forget it: navy blue linen with peasant blouse and peasant skirt with all imported bone lace running through it. When we returned, I decided I was going into Manhattan all decked out in this stunning outfit. My goal was to go into the jewelry salon where my seducer was and seduce him. A new and alluring outfit and a new free-spirited attitude gave me the confidence. With this cocky attitude, I strutted into the salon and boldly walked right up to Kamil and said, "Let's have lunch." He immediately responded "When?" and I blurted out "Now!" We walked out together and went directly across the street to an intimate coffee shop. Nothing fancy, but for me it was, you might say, the womb for my rebirth. He sat across from the table gazing at me intensely with those deep, passionate eyes and with an inviting, sensual smile on his face. My heart immediately came alive. I never realized how long it had been dead. He seemed comfortable and pleased, but I was extremely nervous. He sweetly said, "I want to be with you." Even though this is what I also desired, I froze. In the back of my mind, I knew I needed this one sexual fling. I convinced myself "Just one day. That's all." We planned to meet that following Wednesday at about four in the afternoon at a local hotel in Manhattan. After this brief coffee encounter, I went home filled with guilt. For the next seven days, I couldn't believe what I had decided to do. There were times when I wanted to back out, but something kept pulling me toward him; something was driving me to do this. I'm not sure whether it was depression, loneliness, curiosity, excitement, or the thrill of having someone new, but for whatever reason, I knew I would meet him.

That day, I painstakingly dressed "to the nines" in stiletto heels and drove into the City, leaving behind my beautiful home and secure life in the New Jersey suburbs. When I arrived at the hotel, I reserved a room, as he had told me to do. I went upstairs to the room and anxiously waited for him. He was late, but he finally arrived. Later I learned that he was always late. We had drinks, ate, and had a lively conversation. Clearly, we were both nervous. Then it happened. We were in bed together having wild, untamed sex. We weren't making love; the love came later. The first time we had sex, I must admit that I was disappointed. I thought it would be earth-shattering, phenomenal. I guess we were both frightened; it was new, unfamiliar, and I was a little weird. Kamil was gentle. He was good, but I expected it to be more. We said our goodbyes, and while I was driving back to New Jersey, I became overwhelmed with guilt and began to cry. I knew I was wrong. Yet, I certainly wasn't going to tell my husband the truth. When I got home, I told him I had spent the day with the girls. As usual, David was working at home in his office. After I went up to him and gave him a kiss, I don't know what made me do it, but I said, "Honey, let's make love." He looked at me as if I was crazy. I don't think we were "doing it" even once a week at that time. I put on an alluring nightgown, and we had sex. I recognize now that I was trying to cling onto something, but at that time, I didn't know what. Immediately I realized that what I had done early in the day was wrong, and I decided I wasn't going to do it again – or so I thought. Little did I know that this was the beginning of a clandestine relationship that not only lasted years but has lasted to this very day.

This is a love story about a man whom I worshipped and adored. And even now, he has never been out of my heart. He's a man whom I will love to the day I die. My tale will continue over the next fifteen years.

Chapter Three

DELIGHTFUL AND DANGEROUS FLING

As with many romantic relationships, ours started out with wild passion, playful teasing, secret meetings, clandestine dinners, seductive meetings at intimate cafés, and other contrived liaisons. At first, it was nothing great, nothing unusual – a delightful fling. It didn't start out as a close, authentic relationship. We both had active separate personal lives. We both worked and had private home lives. I was a wife, spent some weekends with my mother, and at times we visited David's daughter. In general, nothing unusual. Fantasy cannot endure when reality exists. Or so I thought!

As Kamil's and my relationship progressed, I pestered him for a position at the jewelry salon. You see, I was tired of commuting back and forth for nonsensical reasons, and I feared David would start to get suspicious. When I first asked Kamil to give me a job at the store, his response was an emphatic, "No"! I guess he wanted to keep his personal life separate from his professional life. At the time, Kamil had no clue that I was a capable salesperson. He viewed me only as a customer, a woman to have fun with.

Kamil was not aware of my prior experience in the industry. At this point, I was just a part-time lover and nothing more. Yet, I was an experienced salesperson. At the age of nineteen, I worked for a high-priced jewelry store near my home. I left that position when I got married and we moved to California where my first husband lived. While I was married to my second husband, David, I worked in boutiques and beauty salons that sold costume jewelry. After much coaxing and begging, Kamil hired me. The real reason I was so insistent and excited about working for Kamil was because I desperately wanted to be closer to him and also to be out of my boring home. New York City was glamorous and fascinating to me. I never gave the long commuting with its heavy traffic a second thought. I viewed it as a wonderful opportunity to spend more time with Kamil, so I totally negated how exhausting it could be. When I first started working, the commute and hours on my feet were exhausting, and I felt disillusioned, but once I walked into the jewelry salon and took one look at my lover, knowing that I would be standing next to him for an entire day, all that was eradicated. To me, all the effort was well worth it.

I vividly and fondly remember the day I first asked him for the job. We were sitting in a small coffee shop. Kamil was wearing this gorgeous gold, diamond-studded pinky ring, a ring he designed and made. I told him how beautiful it was, and he said, "Not as beautiful as you." When Kamil noticed how much I admired it, never taking his eyes off me, he immediately took it off his finger and put it on my finger and whispered, "This is a token of my love for you." The minute I heard those words and felt the ring on my finger, I was filled with ecstasy. He made me feel brand new – as if I was the only woman in the world. It was the first gift he ever gave me, and it will always be memorable and special to me. I was touched because it was given at the spur of the moment, for no special occasion, and to a woman he had only recently met. At that moment, I took advantage of his good nature and asked him for a job. I was heartbroken by his response. He said, "No!" When I retorted "Why not?" Kamil said, "Because it will ruin our relationship." Pleading with him, I said that I would only come in for the Christmas rush – three weeks at the most. He finally agreed, admitting that he could use the help. But first he said that I should go home and ask my husband if it was OK with him. Näively, David agreed.

Chapter Four

DIAMONDS ARE A GIRL'S BEST FRIEND

Every morning during those three weeks of the Christmas rush, when I'd get ready to head into the City, my heart would be beating fast; the pulse of the city was no match for my rapidly beating pulse. I would get up at 7 a.m. every work day and dress carefully, get into my Mercedes, drive over the George Washington Bridge, park at Rockefeller Center, and start my day at the jewelry salon surrounded by sparkling diamonds and my handsome gem of a lover. This was the beginning of a new career and the beginning of a new level in our affair. Little did I know that those three weeks would turn into six incredible yet unsettling years.

My position at the jewelry salon started out as part-time, but it eventually turned into a full-time position. With all my previous experience, I was a dynamo sales person, and both employees and customers loved me. Kamil was impressed; he thought I was terrific. I became his top sales person. "Princess of Madison Avenue" was my nickname. I wore the diamonds and best jewelry as if they were a part of me. I finally had found my knish. Not only did I find my creative talents, but I also found my lover and soul mate. I always loved being surrounded by beautiful, creative people and things. What more could I ask for – I was around the man I was falling in love with, the creative designer of this beautiful jewelry salon, and working side by side.

Kamil loved what he did, and he knew many of the people who came into this store; in time, I got to know them too. Kamil's wife Maria was one of them. During the holidays, when I was working there, she came in with their children. She was meeting Kamil for lunch and holiday shopping. She freely engaged in conversation with the employees while she waited for Kamil. That's how I got to know her and the children.

Chapter Five

BUBBLES, BANGLES AND PARTIES

It was the early 80s and Christmas time, and everyone was in a happy, generous, festive mood. Life was fabulous! Business was good. In the 80s, all those young Wall Street lions were coming into the store to buy diamonds, and money was flowing. Diamond tennis bracelets were a big item – the bigger the diamonds the better. I had just started working for the holiday season, and I absolutely loved it. I came alive and sparkled like the diamonds people were buying and flashing. I couldn't wait to get up in the morning because I knew I was going to a job I loved, being paid well, and near the man who made my heart race uncontrollably.

Kamil loved to party. Being the party person that he was, every day of his life was a party. He could drink a bottle of champagne and chase it down with a bottle of Hennessey whiskey. His eyes glowed, and his face beamed with the brightest smile. One could say that he was a "happy drunk." Every day at noon at the salon, he bought out bottles of cold sparkling champagne for his employees to celebrate life. Then, between four and five, it would start over again. It was an incredibly fun time! We were like one big happy family – in fact, they became my second family. I loved everything about my newfound life. Looking back, I think it was the happiest time of my life. We drank in the afternoon and partied all night. After work, we would go to a bar called Harry's Bar to continue the festivities. My libido became so free that one evening, after someone dared me, I danced on the table at Harry's. Money was being thrown everywhere – they threw one to five dollar bills at me on the table. Remember, I wasn't a kid. I was a married woman in my forties. Yet, I felt the exuberance of frivolous abandonment. I didn't regret it because I was feeling free and happy. Liquor was never my thing; in fact, I didn't drink at all. I was on my own high. Whenever Kamil and I went out for a drink, I ordered a Bloody Mary, took one sip, and that was it. Kamil drank at least five. He would ask me why I would order a drink and never drink it. We were different in so many ways, and yet we were so much alike.

My personality was warm, friendly, and outgoing, and I adored people. But not everyone appreciated me. Throughout my life, many women were jealous of me. I tried not to let that bother me, but, of course, it did, especially over the years. Eventually, I recognized who they were and made a conscious decision to stay away from those people. Now I surround myself only with people I love – the ones who I know care about me. As years pass, you learn that that's what matters most – being around people who truly care about and love you. I had that at the jewelry salon; everyone liked me because I was fun, social, and caring. As far as

I was aware, no one at the store knew about the affair I was having with Kamil. If they did, they never mentioned it, and if they did, I didn't care. I never revealed it to anyone, nor did I flaunt it. This is what Kamil admired about me. In fact, it was many years later before anyone knew about our affair.

There were so many humorous things that happened that first Christmas in the store in the '80s. It was an unusually warm December, and Kamil was in a festive and generous mood. To illustrate his flamboyant nature, he hired an empty truck and had it parked in front of the jewelry salon. Imagine – on a busy street during a hectic time of the year. Inside the truck, he had an abundance of food and drink, and lively music was playing. All the employees from the store were invited to get into the truck where they could eat, drink, and be merry. In other words, to party, and party we did! We were even dancing in the street. But for all the good times at the store, there was the dark side too. People fought and stole, guns were there, FBI investigations – many unusual things happened. Movie stars frequented the store. George Hamilton, Linda Gray, Sylvester Stallone – they spent lots of money, always cash. It was an exciting but unpredictable place to be at. That's what excited me about it. I was always being entertained.

Many people from different countries worked in the industry, and I got to learn all about their fascinating cultures. With Kamil, being Middle Eastern, I got first-hand knowledge of that unique culture. They are very family-oriented, warm, generous, loyal, and fun, and that is how Kamil is.

Another Christmas, Kamil gave a fabulous party in a midtown restaurant for his staff, family, and friends. When the party ended and I was getting ready to leave to go home to David, Kamil told his wife that he was going to walk me out. When we were safely outside, he kissed me, handed me a small pouch, and told me not to open it until I'm in the car. When I opened it, I was thrilled and ecstatic. It was the identical ring that he originally gave me in the coffee shop when we first met. Later that year, on Mother's Day, Kamil gave me a third ring to match the other two. Like me, Kamil is sentimental and those rings represented two people bonding and falling in love. The *trinity* pinky rings became for me the symbol of our abiding friendship, commitment, and love.

The day after Christmas, my husband and I, as we had for many years, left for a week vacation in Aruba with friends. This was the life where I belonged – with my husband and our mutual friends. We had a great time, but I couldn't wait to get back. I longed to return so I could be with my lover and my dynamic new business colleagues

Chapter Six

PERMANENCY AND DOWNFALL

After the New Year, when I returned to work, Kamil asked me if I wanted to work full time. With out the least bit of hesitation, I said, "Yes!" When I told my husband about working full time, he was not happy about it at all. But David knew the kind of person I was and that I was going to do exactly what I wanted to do. I had always been independent, and I refused to be told what to do or what not to do. So I began working five days a week and seven days at Christmas time with the stipulation that I could take off when I needed to. Having proved myself to be a very loyal employee, Kamil knew he could always depend on me. One of my strong points is that I always put my heart and soul into whatever I do, and because of that trait, I became very successful. Kamil paid me well, but eventually it all went back to him. I bought him and his children extravagant gifts for all occasions or even for no occasions. My generosity knew no bounds; I bought for the employees at the store, including Kamil's parents and even his wife, Maria. Everything I did, especially for Kamil, I did from my heart.

Winter turned into spring. Kamil traveled a lot to Europe on business with other men, rarely with his wife. When he returned, he always bought me a gift. Once he surprised me with a magnificent turquoise blue suede coat. I loved it! He had extraordinary taste in both men's and women's clothing. He never liked the way his wife dressed, and he didn't like that she wore no makeup. Frequently and unwisely, he would ask her, "Why don't you dress like Marcia?" I'm sure this didn't bode well with her. That wasn't a smart thing to do because Maria became envious of me. She was jealous of most women. I often wondered if that jealousy was born out of her insecurities created by the fact that many women where attracted to Kamil and showed it. I'm not positive, but my gut feeling believes that this is so.

It is now the spring/summer of 1981, and Kamil was in the process of purchasing a house in Queens for his family. It was not a great house, but he wanted it. He felt it was time to move out of the three-story house where he, Maria, their two children, and his parents were living. After they bought the new house, they gave the old house to his parents, and they rented out the other apartments. The house was in dire need of renovation. Kamil knew I had a background in decorating, and he admired my taste, so he asked me to decorate the new house. He said that if I did the house, I would become a part of it – bringing us closer together. I told my husband that Kamil wanted me to decorate the house for $5,000 and a piece of jewelry. The money was a lie because I would never take money from Kamil. He always gave me jewelry, but I needed an excuse to justify all the jewelry I had accumulated from Kamil and to justify the enormous amount of time I would be spending with my lover. David agreed, and I excitedly accepted the offer. Now my lover and I could spend weekends together with no false excuses and less guilt. This also allowed Kamil to tell his wife we were together doing business without her being suspicious.

It was the summer. Kamil owned a beach house, and that was where Maria and the kids went for the season. It worked out perfectly because he was alone in Queens, and that made it easy for us to be together. We had a ball. We shopped for furniture and for all the items necessary to transform this house into the way he wanted it. In the process, it transformed us – made us not only lovers but respected friends. The house turned out beautiful. The colors were warm brown, ivory, cream, and beige on lacquer. I did the entire downstairs but not the upper level. When Maria came home to see it, she was not satisfied. She claimed it was too modern for her taste, and she didn't like the choice of colors. Kamil loved it, and he told her that it was going to stay. And it did, because Kamil ruled the house.

All summer, while Maria was at the beach and my husband was at home, Kamil and I had a fabulous time being together, not only shopping but having sex every chance we could and everywhere we could, even in the basement. I was filled with excitement. I felt young. I became youthful again, and I looked vibrant. I was falling in love – so in love that words cannot describe it adequately. I would ask Kamil, "Do you love me?" His response was, "Don't I show it to you every day, every night, and every minute that we are together?" In all the years we were together, I think I only heard him say "I love you" two or three times at the most because he thought that words were inadequate and have no meaning, but as a woman, I needed and desperately wanted to hear it. He didn't feel that way; his attitude was to show it, and show it he did. In other words, his motto was "actions speak louder than words." And I guess he did. He did show it numerous times over the years – and in ways other than bedding me down.

Chapter Seven

SEX, LIES, AND LIQUOR
IN THE BIG APPLE

My story is the story of sex, lies, and addictive liaisons in the Big Apple. This is my personal tale of an ambiguous, illicit relationship, of giving and taking – a tale of compassion and passion, generosity, deceit, lies, and lust. Let me assure you, I was not blind to many of Kamil's failures and faults. He certainly was not perfect; he had numerous personality flaws. But love can distort reality, and I must admit that I fell into that category. While I had no illusions about what we were doing and that it was wrong, I was hopelessly obsessed with him. I now recognize that who we fall in love with is beyond our control, no matter how smart and sophisticated we think ourselves.

Some of Kamil's faults were his excessive drinking and his erratic temper. Some might even call him an alcoholic and a hot head. Perhaps he drowned his guilt and insecurities with liquor. In fact, his uncontrollable drinking habit and quick temper got him into trouble not only with his wife but also with others in his everyday life. There were times when he wasn't aware of what he was doing; he would remember it with regret the next day. Sometimes his antics were very funny, but sometimes they were extremely serious; fortunately, or unfortunately, he never went to jail or seriously hurt himself or anyone else.

We tried to be very discreet about our rendezvous in the Big Apple, but at times this was almost impossible. In our second year, we accidentally ran into his uncle at the hotel. Because family honor is so important in his culture, Kamil was extremely upset that his uncle had seen us. During his drive back home alone that night, someone hit the back of his Bentley. He immediately jumped out of the car and ran over and kicked the car of the other person and broke his own ankle. He called me the next day and told me how he had gotten hurt. He said that tempers were flying and that due to his uncontrollable temper; he had broken his ankle and had to be taken to the hospital. He told his wife that he fell into a pothole. Kamil was always getting hurt; he was what you might call a real klutz. He frequently hammered his finger while working on jewelry; he was always bandaged. In my blindness to his faults, I found this cute.

By this time, our sex life was incredible, yet we were also bonding on so many other levels. We fit together like a glove. Kamil and I both loved to dance and our life together was like an untamed tango. During 1981-82, we were both invited to many social events. Kamil went with Maria, and I went with David. Kamil loved to celebrate at these events by drinking Ouzo. Let me warn you, Ouzo hits you like a ton of bricks. Thankfully, my husband and I didn't drink, but Maria and Kamil did, and Maria got deathly sick from it at one event. She was so ill that she had to run into the bathroom. I followed her in and held her head while she was throwing up in the toilet. How many women do you know who would hold the head of their lover's wife while she was puking in the toilet? Yet, there I was. Maria was so out of it that she didn't recall a thing. I did it because Kamil asked me to, and that is exactly what I did – I did it for him. At the time, my love was in blind obedience for him. Perhaps you can say I was addicted to him. He was my aphrodisiac drug of choice and I could not kick the habit.

Chapter Eight

FOUR BY FOUR IS A CROWD
BUT TWO BY TWO IS SUBLIME

This is a tale of a relationship between four people: my husband, my lover, his wife, and me. We socialized together at special events and also went out for intimate dinners together. My husband and I were frequently invited to their house. I must admit I dragged my reluctant husband. I insisted, claiming that he was my boss – this excuse always worked. I desperately wanted to be in their home, the home I had decorated and the home where his beloved children were. There were times when I tucked his two young children to bed and read them bedtime stories. I felt I needed to be integrated into his life. His kids and I got very close, and they eventually called me Aunt Marcia. I showered them with gifts, especially at Christmas. I began to believe that they were not only Kamil's children but mine as well. Since I had no children of my own, I felt a burning desire to be an intricate part of my lover's children's lives. In fact, during the holidays when he was busy at work, he gave me money to go out and buy gifts for his wife and kids. I bought his wife many luxurious gifts. I did everything he asked me to do. I didn't mind because it made him happy, and that made me happy. I wanted to make him happy because I sensed so much unhappiness in him. He had a great sadness deep inside. Kamil wanted so much more out of life, and he was held back. I believe he was unfulfilled in his marriage and yearned for a deep, loving relationship. I know that that is what drew us closer together – both of us needed to be loved unconditionally.

It was easy being a warm, generous person to Kamil because he brought it out in me. When I was with him, no matter what he did, I would forgive him. Looking back, perhaps, it was a fault of mine, a sickness, but I didn't care. I denied and defied everyone and everything for him.

In the fall of 1981, we had been together for over a year. Things were good. My job was great, and we were happy. In fact, all four of us were content. No one was getting hurt, or so we rationalized. We were having our clandestine affair, a sizzling love affair, and seeing each other as much as possible. We had a routine. Kamil and I went to our favorite haunt every day after work for a drink. It was easy for me because traffic leaving New York City at 6 p.m. was impossible, so I had the believable excuse of leaving after the traffic died down. I was getting home around 8 p.m. three or four times a week. We would even meet for breakfast before work. After work, we had dinner at some of New York's finest spots. La Reserve, right around the corner, or at Rockefeller Center, where in the winter we watched the ice skaters, or at the outdoor café in the summer. These were our alone, happy times, our time to talk about everything excluding business or spouses. Those topics were taboo. Every opportunity we had, we went to various hotels and motels in New York, New Jersey, and Long Island, even on weekends. It would be impossible to say how many times. It was never enough for us. We couldn't get enough of one another. We were dangerously delirious for one another.

One time when my husband was in Florida visiting his mother and Maria was in Europe, Kamil and I had an entire night to be alone together without the concern of our spouses. Making love all night, I climaxed three times, which had never happened to me in my entire life, and he came seven times that night. It was reckless abandonment. I can't recall ever having so much sex before; whenever he was ready, I was ready, even when it was that time of month. It didn't matter. I never said *no* to him. He intoxicated me. That morning, as a concerned father, Kamil left the hotel at 4:30 a.m. to go back home so when his children woke up, he could be there to get them ready for school. Just to show how crazy he was, when he got them off to school, he slept for two hours and then drove back to the hotel to be with me again.

Chapter Nine

DECEIT, INDISCRETION, DEATH, AND REVELATION

After our sexual encounters, sometimes Kamil would stay in the city and sleep over at his friend Lorenzo's place. Maria knew they were long-time buddies, and it gave Kamil an excuse not to go home when he didn't want to go or if he was angry with his wife. Lorenzo's couch was always available to Kamil. They were great drinking buddies. Lorenzo could drink Kamil under the table, and to this day he still does. One time when Kamil and Lorenzo had to fly somewhere they asked me to drive them to the airport. When we got to Lorenzo's apartment we thought we had time so we started to party and dance. I danced with such fervor that the top of my dress came off exposing my flying breasts. I felt like one of Botticelli's beautiful topless muses and not a cheap stripper because I was in love. Without even drinking, Kamil intoxicated me and spurred me on. We became so out-of-control that we lost track of time and they missed their flight. Kamil and Lorenzo were such good friends that Kamil crashed at his apartment many times. I couldn't because I had to go back to my husband prepared with every excuse I could come up with for being late. Kamil taught me how to lie with a straight face to my husband and told me never to admit anything, and I never did!

My husband David died in 1989, and I never revealed my affair to him. He never knew about my love for Kamil. Or if he *did* know, he never let on that he did, and I never gave him reason to think otherwise. As far as I can discern, he died never knowing about my indiscretions or that I had fallen in love with another man – a man we were both socially active with and whom both of us considered a friend.

The year 1982 was a strange year, an extremely sad and reveal-ing year for me. My life took a major pivotal turn. The most profound event was the sudden death of my dear father and the untimely illness of my mother. Out of this sadness, my relation-ship with Kamil took a different turn. This is where my sexual desire for Kamil turned to a deep abiding love and cemented my admiration for him. I started to see the compassion and inner beauty of my lover. He was by my side through the death of my father and the illness of my mother. After all that happened that year, I realized how much I truly loved Kamil. He revealed a side of himself that I hadn't seen before. Prior to these life-altering events, he was just someone to have fun with, to make me feel alive, and to make me feel like a beautiful, sensuous woman. Even to this day, I saw in him something that I had not seen in anyone before that I was involved with.

This transformation began on a beautiful fall day in New York City. I was working at the jewelry salon when I got a call from my niece that my father had been rushed to the hospital with a heart attack. I turned to Kamil and said, "My dad is going to die." He told me not to be ridiculous and to go to the hospital and I'd see then that all would be fine. Even with these reassuring words, I knew in my heart that my father wouldn't make it. My father had been playing golf when he began to have chest pains. He was 78 years old, and, up to this point, he had never been sick a day in his life. When I got to the hospital in New Jersey, he was still alive. My mother and half-sister were there. At first the prognosis was somewhat hopeful. My dad, who was a dentist and had medical knowledge, said that on a scale from 1-10 his heart attack was a 6. To this day, I can still visualize every tube that was in him and the fearful look in his eyes. When you lose someone you love dearly, you remember mostly the very last time you saw her or him. With deep pain and fear in my heart, I went home to my husband. While I was home, the phone rang. I knew immediately that my father had passed away. My father died on October 6, 1982. This was the first painful death I had to endure, and it was excruciating for me. I loved my father dearly, and he loved me. I was devastated!

My dad was a strong, stern man who commanded respect, but he was a very good person. He took great care of me, and I could depend on him. He always looked after me, and now, he was gone. To this day I miss him terribly. The funeral was on the eighth. In the Jewish religion, we celebrate the day they are buried. In the funeral parlor, I was hysterical, crying uncontrollably. No one could comfort me. My husband was not by my side – I had no idea where David was. Kamil and his wife were invited to the services, but I did not see them. I wondered where they were. But when we got to the cemetery, there was Kamil and his wife. He never disappointed me. He immediately came up to me and gave me his heartfelt condolences. Kamil whispered in my ear that they had gotten lost and had had to bypass the funeral parlor.

After the cemetery, we went to my mother's apartment that over looked my beloved Manhattan. Everyone was there, including Kamil and Maria. People chattered discreetly and partook of the lavish table of food items that friends had brought. Through my teary eyes, I noticed Kamil talking with my mother. They had met before when my parents had come to the jewelry salon to buy jewelry. Once, my father had come to the store to have a gold coin made into a necklace for my mother. My father never surmised that Kamil and I were lovers, but my mother did. She later said she could tell just by the way we looked at each other.

In the Jewish religion, we sit Shiva for a week. Every day, Kamil attended. One day, while we were sitting Shiva, my mother complained of a terrible headache. I felt it was no big deal, especially under the circumstances with all the pressure she was under – and my mother was a bit of a hypochondriac. Another day, when the house was full, while Kamil was sitting next to my mother, her headache resumed. In fact, it became more intense and unbearable. So much so that we had to call 911. My mother was rushed to the same hospital where my father had just died a few days before. After extensive tests, they discovered that my mother had a blood clot, an embolism, on her brain. My half-sister Rene and I had to make a life-threatening decision as what to do. Remember, my father had died just five days before; I had lost ten pounds and was not in a sound frame of mind. I became physically and mentally paralyzed. I became incapable of making a rational decision. We had two choices. Have them operate on her or leave it alone and let fate take its course. She could become brain dead through the surgery, or we could leave it be and take our chances. We painstakingly decided to leave it alone. Let her die in peace, we thought, and not put her through the pain of surgery. My mother was in the hospital for twenty-eight days. I went every day. My husband came now and then; eventually, he stopped coming. Yet my loving and compassionate Kamil came nightly after work to sit with my mother and hold her hand. Kamil wore this large gold and diamond cross on his neck. My mother admired it, even though Jewish people didn't believe in it; yet she believed in God, so he gave it to her to hold. She held onto the cross, and she felt that is what kept her alive. Later, he made a duplicate of that same cross and gave it to my mother, telling her that it symbolized friendship and faith. Here was a total stranger giving my mother something from the bottom of his heart. My mother clung to that cross, and for whatever reason, she survived. Thankfully, after twenty-eight days, the embolism dissolved. My mother wore that cross until the day she died, some ten years later. Kamil's acts of kindness and generosity changed my love for him from a sexual love into a deeper, more-endearing one filled with respect and admiration.

Prior to these events, late October, I had planned a surprise 50th birthday party for my husband in Atlantic City. Everything was set. I invited eight couples, all high rollers. Kamil and his wife were also invited. Remarkably, even at this party, Kamil and I managed to make love at the hotel pool after our spouses went to bed. We didn't return to our rooms until 3 a.m. Earlier, when I told my mother that I was going to cancel the party, she insisted that I shouldn't. She said that my father would have wanted me to have it as she did. My mother was a considerate person. She was a gorgeous petite woman and was more beautiful than I am. My mother had a great personality, and was an elegant, immaculate dresser, and I inherited those traits from her.

Chapter Ten

MOTHERS, DAUGHTERS AND LOVER

They say that mothers' and daughters' relationships can be very complex, and that is exactly how I perceive my relationship with my mother. I have ambiguous feelings about our mother/daughter relationship. My mother cared for and loved her daughters. But I never knew my mother intimately. There was never any understanding between us. For whatever reason, I never felt close to her. Maybe because she worked for my dad for forty years and was never home when I returned from school. I don't know. I could never figure it out. There was a tremendous void between my mother and myself. Yet Kamil seemed to understand her. She adored him, maybe because she saw how he treated me. My mother noticed his caring nature and his intense warmth and compassion toward others. They had a strong bond that lasted for many years until just a few years before she died, which was the last time she saw him.

He always called her, he always cared, and these are the things that I loved most about him. He always took the time for others. I remember one incident when we were going to Long Island by ourselves, our spouses were away. In the car, he said, "Let's call Mom. She's alone, and I want to see if she's OK." Even when she moved to Florida, he checked up on her. He sent her flowers and cards for her birthday, for Mother's Day, or for no reason – this was who he was. Because Mom was a part of my life, he made her a part of his life too. He had "heart," and he showed it, especially to me. That's why I adored him.

Chapter Eleven

"MARRIAGE, SECRETS, AND DECEPTION GO TOGETHER LIKE A WOLF IN SHEEP'S CLOTHING"

My second husband, David, and I where married in 1973. But prior to our marriage, he told everyone that we had been married November 30, 1972. The truth of the matter is, we got married March 30, 1973. Not intentionally, but I think that is when lying became a part of my life, although I truly believe that it began in my childhood. I hide behind everything, as did my mother. For example, I never knew that my mother was married before she married my father. My half-sister Rene was born out of this marriage. I didn't find out about this until I was sixteen years old. Can you imagine – one day while I was at the country club with my friends, a classmate said to me that there was a rumor going around about my mother having been married before my father and that Rene was the child from that prior marriage. Vehemently I denied it and went home and confronted my mother, and she finally acknowledged it. I felt totally betrayed. All those years, and I was never told. My mother was living a lie.

Perhaps her lie taught me to manipulate the truth and be secretive. I always had the attitude to keep things a secret. In fact, I kept a lot of unpleasant things inside of me assuming that they would go away if I ignored and didn't address them. Because of this, I didn't trust many people.

At the age of fourteen, I fell in love – at least I thought it was love – with an unlikely person. Franco was an Italian man with Mafia connections. It could never work out, but for years I pined for him. Fifteen years later, when I was married to my first husband and living in California, I still felt I was in love with Franco. Looking back, there were countless men in my life, but none who really captured my heart. I was fickle. I had wild crushes. I cared for many, and at times, I thought I was in love. Perhaps I was – you know, young, carefree, and had innocent infatuations. During those youthful years, every one is in love, including me. But did I really know what love was? I certainly went for all the wrong men. Until I met Kamil – or so I thought. Before him, I only went through the motions, doing all the right things that society dictated, such as dating someone like yourself, marrying someone your own age, and starting a family together.

With my first husband, Keith, I had three miscarriages. One of them was with twins. Was I ready to have children then, or was I still a child myself? Besides, I never loved Keith. I married him on a rebound. I had no feelings for him. The very night of our wedding, I knew it was the biggest mistake of my life. Our courtship was a whirlwind. I met him at the Catskills, dated him for three months, and foolishly married him. Strange, I married

Keith and David on the same day but with a ten-year span. I made the same mistake exactly ten years later on the same date – March 30, 1963, and March 30, 1973. I didn't realize that until years later. History repeats itself. We make the same foolish mistakes. My first husband was also cold and calculating, and I didn't love him, but he was rich, very rich, and I thought I could grow to love him. I didn't know what I was doing. I think I liked the idea of living in Beverly Hills and the so-called glamour that goes with it – all the excitement being around the movie industry. When do we learn?

Keith's mother and father were divorced, and his biological mother was married to an entertainment lawyer. She was married so many times that I couldn't keep track of her husbands. She was married to the entertainment lawyer when I was married to Keith, and frequently when I visited them at their house with its magnificent pool, many famous movie stars were present. Fifties stars such as Robert Culp, Vince Edwards, Barry Sullivan, plus many more. So I had a first-hand taste of being surrounded by big-name celebrities and what that lifestyle was all about. That's when my lies began to resurface.

Having absolutely no loving feelings toward him whatsoever, I married Keith under false pretense. I was so unhappy; I was alone in a strange, plastic city. When I first found out I was pregnant, I didn't even know if the marriage would last.

When I was first married to David, I had a crush on Aldo, my hairdresser at the time. Hairdressers seem to turn me on. Aldo was my first mature crush. I used to go into his salon looking sexy and lure him into have lunch with me. Imagine, I spent two to three hours in the salon just to have my short hair blown out. I had a thing for him, but again he was married with four children and unattainable. Do you see the pattern here? He loved to talk sexy and dirty, and I played into it. Looking back, I realize that I was doing things I should never have been doing. You see, like Keith, I didn't love David either. I cared about him and also married him because he was a challenge and I wanted to conquer him. I always went for the guy who gave me some excitement. Perhaps I fell for Kamil also because he was unattainable and a challenge. We were both married; he was young, gorgeous, and dangerous. But it was wrong!

There I was again repeating the same destructive patterns of lies and deceit and having illicit affairs. I was always cheating. Was I doing it for the sex? I don't think so. I'm sexual, but I'm not crazy. It was the dare that seduced me. Kamil was a huge challenge. Even before I loved him, I wanted Kamil to fall madly and hopelessly in love with me. Is it part of my self-destructive personality? If people said *no* to me, I had to get them to say *yes*. I'm not sure where this comes from. Was it because I was always searching for the unattainable to prove something to me? I had no clue as to what it was. Was I searching for the "Knight in Shinning Armor" to take me away from everything? But from what!

As I mentioned earlier, Kamil, Maria, David, and I did everything together. But Kamil and I spent a lot of time alone. Did anyone suspect? Perhaps so, but no one ever gave us an inkling that they did. No one ever came up to me and suggested or accused me of it. Once a friend of mine said that her husband saw me at a ball game with Kamil, but that's it. As time went on, it got easier; we began to let our guard down. In fact, when David was in Brooklyn playing cards, which he did once or twice a week, Kamil came over to the house and we made love in the same bed in which David and I shared. We took risks but ignored them since we had been getting away with it for so long. By turning a blind eye, David always confused and stymied me. Did he do it on purpose?

Kamil and I were very much alike in these matters. He was cheating long before I came into the picture. I wasn't his first, and I certainly wasn't his last. I'm not naïve. Most likely, when he traveled to the Bahamas or to Europe with the guys, there were other women. Kamil frequently went to Jamaica with the guys, and his philosophy was, "I always do what I want!" He didn't give a crap about his wife as long as she was home taking care of his kids. Was he a male chauvinist? By today's standards, absolutely! I remember once when he came back from the islands, Club Med, with his buddies, he brought back photos of them all screwing an Island girl. I took one look at the pictures and I knew it was Kamil. I confronted him, and he said it wasn't him. I said, "Don't fool me. That's your ass – I'd know it anywhere." He knew I knew, but it didn't matter because casual sex wasn't love; it was just someone miles away. He was having cheap fun, I rationalized. Actually, I didn't give a damn about it; I knew it was nothing serious. But, if he did it in front of me, like someone from New York or at the jewelry salon, and if I found out he was sleeping with another woman whom he might love, that would be totally another story. Love is blind; perhaps I wanted to believe his cheap antics were nothing. Yet, truthfully, I believe that in all the years we were together, he was pretty faithful. For some reason, he thought that he wasn't my first affair even though I lied and told him that he was. Did we lie to one another? Absolutely! Kamil was not my first affair, and I wasn't his.

Chapter Twelve
AN AFFAIR TO DENY OR AN
AFFAIR TO TREASURE?

When I was in California and was married to my first husband, Keith, I did have an affair. Yet Kamil thought it was with Aldo, my hairdresser from New Jersey. When he asked me, I could look him directly in the eye and deny it, shouting back, "Absolutely not!" My moral conscious was clear. It wasn't happening and it never happened; I wish it had happened at that time. As far as our lovemaking went, Kamil and I were great together. It was the best. For me, he was the ultimate. Not because of the sex but because of the way he treated me. I'll always remember the way I fit into his arms after we made love. Sometimes we lay there together for an hour or two. I will always treasure and recall the tender and passionate way he touched and kissed me. He was not only physically tender to me but also emotionally available for me, unlike my husband, David.

For example, in 1981, my husband David and I were heading into New York to visit my parents for the High Jewish holiday, Yom Kippur. In route, a car sideswiped us and I was badly bruised, and terribly frightened. In fact, police cars and an ambulance were immediately called to the accident. I was black and blue, broke all of my nails, and had whiplash, but more so, I was terrified of David's selfish, erratic behavior. After the impact, he didn't bother to see if I was hurt, he jumped out of the car and began to rant and rave about how his new Mercedes was damaged. He was not one bit concerned about my well being or even his. When I returned to work that Monday and Kamil saw how bruised I was, he hugged me and gently kissed all of the areas of my body that were hurt and held me in his arms as I cried, not over my physical pain but over the emotional pain that David inflicted on me. Kamil's overwhelming compassion was a glaring contrast to David's blatant disregard. Clearly, my husband's inability to acknowledge my pain was more damaging than what I received from the accident.

To emphasize David's lack of concern and compassion, in 1985, I needed a hysterectomy. This was the critical turning point in my relationship with David. I went to Columbia Presbyterian Hospital in New York to have the surgery. My recovery period was an entire week. When I first came out of surgery, someone was putting cold ice chips on my parched lips. Slowly I opened my eyes, thinking I'd see my husband, but it was not David. It was Kamil. The doctor came in to see how I was doing. I sensed that he was taken aback by seeing someone gently kissing my forehead and putting ice on my lips, distracting me from my pain by talking to me soothingly – and it wasn't my husband. The doctor never suspected or, did he?

The next day, my friend Anna came to visit. David came right after her. He wasn't even present for my operation. He was in Atlantic City. Anna was disturbed to see that when David came in the room, he didn't give me a hug or a kiss. He didn't bring me flowers or even ask how I was feeling. Needless to say, this upset me terribly also. I told David that I was desirous of something other than bland hospital food – like a grilled cheese sandwich. This truly was not a lot to ask. He responded back in an angry voice, "I just got here, and I'm not going out again. I'd never find another parking space." Anna sharply replied back, "David, she's hungry. Go out and get her something to eat!" I looked at David, and I knew at that moment that I had no love whatsoever for this selfish man. This feeling would be reaffirmed a week later while I was recuperating at our house.

You can say that life begins to unravel in one area and yet becomes tighter in other areas. This was beginning to happen. My life with David, independently of the affair, had been unraveling for a number of years. And my affair with Kamil was becoming more secure and more loving. One night while I was recovering and David and I were home, I was sitting by the living room window working on a jigsaw puzzle, one with the illustration of jewelry. I happened to gaze out the window, and I was shocked and thrilled to see Kamil walking up our driveway with a huge bouquet of flowers in his arms. This was a total surprise. I had no idea that he was coming. When the doorbell rang, my heart leaped for joy. David opened the door, and I could hear Kamil tell him that he was in the area visiting with relatives and wanted to stop by and see how I was doing. David cautiously but cordially invited him in. When Kamil came into the living room, I saw in his eyes that he longed to see me and to find out how I was feeling. There we were, the three of us, my husband, my lover, and I, a love triangle, spending time together talking and kibitzing. Was David aware of our affair? If he was, he never gave a clue. Did Kamil and I care? Not a bit. Kamil and our affair became more than a sexual arrangement at this time. He worried about me, he wanted to make me happy, and he showed his love by going outside the bed and into my heart. When he left, I felt sad, but I was no longer lonely because he was permanently in my heart. At this point, David was evicted from my heart by his cruelty and lack of concern for me both physically and emotionally – an emotional abandonment that started long before Kamil entered my life.

During my recuperation period, I had a nurse with me during the day before I had the staples taken out of my stomach. When the nurse was relieved of her duties, I still needed assistance. One day when I needed help taking a shower, I asked David. All he had to do was walk me to the shower, assist me in, and hold me. He refused because he said he couldn't look at my stomach because, he implied, it looked disgusting. That hurt me deeply. A week after the surgery, during the summer, I had to go to the doctor in New York and have the staples removed. I made the appointment for the following Tuesday. When David came home that night, I asked politely, "Honey, I made the appointment for next Tuesday to see the doctor, and I need you to drive me into the city." To this day, I will never forget his response. He nonchalantly and coolly responded, "I can't." When I questioned him as to why not, he sarcastically replied that he had another appointment for that day. Even after pleading with him, he told me to make other arrangements. The day of the appointment, alone and ailing, I took an hour-long cab ride in extreme heat into New York. When I arrived at the doctor's office, the nurse asked me where my husband was and who had accompanied me. I began to cry. The nurse informed me that I needed to call someone because I could not go home alone. Of course, I called Kamil. I was uptown and he was downtown. He asked me where I was, and I told him I was in the doctor's office. He heard me crying. He said, "What's going on? I told him I had had the staples taken out of my stomach, and he asked, "Where is David?" I said he wasn't with me. Kamil said, without hesitation, "I'll be there in ten minutes." He came to the doctor's office, put me in his car, and drove me back to New Jersey.

When I walked into the house with Kamil, it was almost dinnertime, and David was home. When he saw us come in together, he asked us what we were doing. I told him I took a cab alone to Manhattan to the doctor's and Kamil took me home. I said he was staying for dinner. The three of us sat in the back patio sharing dinner, and David acted as if nothing happened. He never even asked how I was doing or apologized for not accompanying me, nor did he thank Kamil for bringing me home. His cold aloofness was so apparent that it was unnerving and revealing. I knew at that moment that my marriage was over. There would be no discussion to the contrary. I didn't care about the consequences, I didn't care about the trauma, and I didn't care where I was going to live. I just knew it was over. I glanced into the eyes of the two men sitting next to me – my husband and my lover. David's eyes were empty, and Kamil's were filled with love and compassion. When he had seen me for the first time with the staples in my stomach, I didn't want to show him, so I put my hands over my stomach. Kamil made me take my hands away and gently kissed it. In complete contrast, my husband had turned away from me and called my temporarily deformed stomach disgusting. They say that you can see the soul of a person through their eyes. I had an epiphany. It was at that precise moment that I decided to leave David. Did I jump from the frying pan into the fire? That remains to be told.

Chapter Thirteen

DOUBTS, REGRETS, AND REGRESSION

This story is not only about my love affair with Kamil but also about my life after him. This relationship lasted over twenty years. We broke up after six years. This is a story about survival, compassion, caring, financial support, and everything I shared with Kamil from the moment in 1985 when I left my husband, David. Kamil always asked me the question, even a few years back, "Would you have divorced David if I wasn't in the picture?" I always told him, "I *would* have divorced David anyway." Another lie because, most likely, in retrospect, I would not have. It had nothing to do with how happy I was; it was about having a husband, being married, having mutual friends, and traveling together. I would be willing to go through even the unhappy moments of sharing financial concerns such as David's gambling, our debts, and all the other negative things. I now believe that as we got older, David and I could have mellowed and accepted our faults and could have stayed together like so many other long-term married couples. But this would not be. Kamil changed all that.

David was cheating on me. I knew it, but I didn't care because I had my own lover. David was seen many times in Atlantic City with a blonde woman who eventually became his fifth wife. They were married a very short time before he died. Many people saw them together, including my own sister Rene, who told me. Yet, it didn't matter. Why didn't I feel anything? Why didn't I say to him what are you doing? The answer is simple – because I didn't want him to confront me with what I was doing. As they say, what is good for the goose is good for the gander. But I believed that there was no question in my mind as to who had the affair first? I'm sure I was. I believe I started with Kamil long before David went outside our marriage, even before David was cheating with this girlfriend-at-the-time whom he met at a shop where he purchased his clothes. I just didn't care. I was happy. My life was good; I had my home, I had material things, I had my sexy young boyfriend, and I had a fulfilling job that I absolutely adored. The work was tiring, but it was fun and very exciting.

I fondly remember the night just before David and I were getting ready to leave for Florida to meet a cruise ship to go on a holiday with friends. Kamil told me we were going to the Waldorf Astoria. I asked him why we were going there. He told me we were going to the penthouse to sell jewelry to the Hiltons, not Paris and Nikki but their parents. We went over there that night, and Kamil was very drunk but having fun. I was in a private bedroom in the hotel selling jewelry to the older Hilton sisters and the family. Nikki and Paris weren't even born then. I sold one hundred thousand dollars worth of jewelry that night. Afterwards, we left the hotel and began walking back to the jewelry salon. Kamil wanted to put the jewelry that wasn't sold back into the safe. It was almost midnight. I called David and told him what I was doing and he was extremely angry, but at this point, I didn't care. I was doing what I wanted to do, as I always did. This is how Kamil and I are alike. We were so hot for one another that we didn't even wait to get to the shop so we stopped at an alcove of a darkened building and screwed our brains out – in the middle of the street at midnight. This is what we did, crazy things in crazy places. Then, I nonchalantly got myself together and went home.

When I arrived home, David was furious. He was always angry with me, but he never did anything about it. Maybe I wanted him to throw something at me or put his fist through the wall. I don't know what I wanted him to do. I never got a reaction from him, and that was probably one of the problems in our marriage. Even when I asked him for a divorce, he never showed any emotion. Was he also hiding behind all of his feelings? I believe that was part of it. Did he not care at that point? Probably not, but he never confronted me, he never asked, he never accused. In fact, the next day we got on the plane together and went to Florida to go on the cruise with our friends. I remember another time when we were in Florida. David had a convention to attend, and I accompanied him. I was with David at the convention booth, and when he left to check on something, I called Kamil in New York. When he answered, I started to cry hysterically. When he asked me what was wrong, I told him I missed him terribly. I only wanted to be back in the City; I only wanted to be back at work; I only wanted to be at his side. I was starting to fall apart. Things were starting to get to me; I was depressed, I was not happy in my marriage – I just wanted to spend more time with Kamil at any cost.

Chapter Fourteen

I CAN DEPEND ON YOU AND YOUR GENEROSITY

Kamil never let me down. At Christmas, he took me out before he went home to his family. The only time we were not together was on New Year's Eve, and that was impossible for me since David I went to Aruba every New Years with friends. There wasn't a holiday that Kamil skipped. Whether it was Mother's Day, Christmas, Easter, my birthday, his birthday, we were always together. We were always celebrating. He showered me with gifts; I have so many gifts from him. The jewelry alone is not to be believed. I wish I had it today, but later, as things got bad for me, I had to sell most of it. I sold one piece at a time. Some of the gifts he gave me are four carat pave-diamond earrings; ruby and diamond heart double rings; an 18 carat solid gold key chain with diamond heart in the center saying "I love my Jaguar," which I owned in 1986; an 18 carat gold love bracelet with diamonds; a cuff bracelet with diamonds, sapphires, and rubies; yellow topaz and diamond earrings; and my three diamond rings that I still have today. Those rings will go to my grave with me because they are the only pieces I have left from Kamil. As far as I am concerned, they represent our wedding bands. I wore them for years. He also gave me an 18 carat gold necklace that weighed a ton with 10 diamonds in it. All these pieces he made and gave me over the years. Kamil made and gave me anything I ever wanted, and I never asked for any them. He always surprised me.

Sadly, I can't recall anything that David bought me. I always had to go and get it myself. He never took the time. I never wore a wedding band, and I never had an engagement ring in my life. I wore a diamond pear-shaped engagement and a diamond wedding band, but they were all imitation – CZs as they say in the jewelry business. To this day, I do not have a thing that David ever bought me. Nothing! It was as if the seventeen years that I was with him never existed. Yet, I still remember and treasure everything Kamil gave me, even clothing – suede jackets, silk blouses, and purses he bought me from Europe. I, in turn, gave to him. He loved Elvis Presley, so I gave him an original work of art of Elvis by the famous artist Hirschfeld, which he still has to this day. I gave him a first edition of an Elvis Presley doll, which I'm sure he still treasures. I gave him authentic Louis Vuitton luggage. I bought him a mink jacket and countless other gifts. I just couldn't do enough, couldn't spend enough. It didn't matter what it took. For his thirty-fifth birthday, I bought him a special watch. He had a very small wrist, and he adored this special white gold watch. I bought it for him, and he truly loved it. But he lost it – it fell off his wrist in Manhattan, and it was never recovered.

Chapter Fifteen

HOW MUCH IS THAT DOGGIE IN THE WINDOW? TOO MUCH?

Kamil revealed his soft side many times when he cried. When his kids were small, he wanted to buy them a puppy. One day, we went to a pet store and got an adorable Miniature Collie. He said he wanted that particular one because it had red hair like me. Kamil took it home, and the kids were so excited; they loved that puppy. They had it for a few months, and then one day Kamil came into the salon, and he was crying. When I asked him why he was crying, he told me that Maria had insisted that he get rid of the dog and that he had just gotten back from the pound. She wanted him to tell the children that the dog had gotten killed. I think that was the first time I ever saw hatred in Kamil's eyes toward another human being – and it was his wife. He was devastated because his kids were so unhappy and because the puppy meant so much to him and because we had purchased it together. I loved it also, as did his kids. When he realized what he had done, and when he realized that his wife was being a complete selfish bitch, he tried to get the dog back, but the dog had already been given away. He said that he hoped it was given to a good family. That was the end of our adorable puppy. Maria didn't want to be bothered taking care of the dog, and she made him the heavy by making him give it away and explain it to his children with a lie.

Theirs was a strange household. I remember one day while I was at the house, after I had decorated it, Maria was at the beach, and we decided to go to the bedroom to have sex. When I entered the room, I was shocked by the color of the room. The entire bedroom was painted with dark and gloomy colors. I shouted, "What did you do?" He said, " I did this because this is how I feel." He put in black tile floors; he painted the walls a morbid color. Everything in the room was dark, including the furniture. The only items that were white were the sheets. I couldn't believe it. I suddenly realized what his life was really like. Despite all the bravado, he was not happy; he lived a dismal personal existence.

Our relationship was a very unusual one. Many people have sexual affairs, but this is not what our relation was all about. It was about the incredible connection between two human beings who came from extremely different walks of life. We came to-gether as soul mates, confidants, business partners, and with trust in and respect for one another. It was a friendship that would last for many, many years of turmoil and love. Kamil gave me financial support even after we broke up. He never let me down; he was always there for me. And that was the strange part of this relationship. As the years went by, he continued to be there for me; if I asked for anything, he gave it to me; if I needed anything, he gave it. The incredible thing was that he never asked any questions. He never asked, "Why do you need this"? "Why do you want that?" Did he do it out of guilt after our break up or for screwing up my life totally? I'll never know.

Chapter Sixteen

LOVE, LOSS, HEART BREAK, AND LIFE AFTER

But even with this generosity and friendship, Kamil made it impossible for me to ever have a decent relationship with another man. He made it impossible for me to commit to or be married to anyone again. He permanently ruined my future romantic life. I believe that he is astutely aware that he destroyed my ability to relate to another person on a romantic level. Was that why he continued to give me financial assistance and benign friendship? Is he consumed with guilt? Only Kamil can answer that question.

I don't think most people can even image or understand what it is like, year after year, going to bed with different men in hopes of finding that perfect connection. In hopes of finding someone to replace that perfect lover and soul mate. While I was in bed, having sex with another man, I wound up crying, because all I thought about was Kamil. No man could compare to him. The heartbreak has forever altered me and was unbearable; he was a scar on my heart; a permanent one. As an intelligent woman, I knew this wasn't normal. Even after all my years in therapy, nothing helped. My therapists always told me that I had to let go and that Kamil was not good for me. I knew they were right. I was keenly aware that I had to let go, and trust me, I tried. I began by not calling him, by throwing away things that reminded me of him, personal things. You can do all those things, but you can't throw away your mind or repair a broken heart, and that is where the problem lies. It wasn't my style to deal with my pain by using alcohol or drugs. It seems as if I wanted to live with the pain. I kept asking myself, was I punishing myself for ruining my own life, my marriage, for destroying everything and everyone around me? And, more importantly, for ending up alone all these years. It's easy to blame someone else for your problems and making excuses, but in reality, I did it myself. I put myself in this position; no one else put me there. I was my judge and my jury. I put myself through my own personal hell.

Chapter Seventeen

WALLOWING IN DANTE'S INFERNO

Hell. How do you describe hell? When did I fall into the deep abyss of hell? I guess we can start by exploring how our relationship began to unravel, eventually leading to a break up. I was forty-five, and Kamil and I had already been together for over five years. I couldn't endure my marriage with David any longer. It was my birthday, and David and I were going out to celebrate. David and I were meeting friends of ours at a very fine French restaurant in Manhattan. We were driving from New Jersey over the George Washington Bridge. The magnificent New York skyline mesmerized me. Ironically, with that romantic backdrop, I nonchalantly turned to David and said, "I want a divorce." He turned around and said to me, "Are you crazy?" and I calmly responded, "No, I need to be separated from you; I need some space; I need time to think." Nothing more was said in the car that night. We got into New York and met our friends at the restaurant. We were sitting down at the table, and we were having a wonderful dinner. It's my birthday! I look gorgeous. All of a sudden, out of the blue, out of my mouth comes, "David and I are getting a divorce." I thought my friends would fall right off their chairs and onto the floor. They were shocked! Actually, when everyone found out, they were all shocked.

We came home that night, and there was still no reaction from my husband. David wasn't mad; he wasn't excitable. He casually commented, "What do you want to do?" I suggested that since we had a place in Aruba and we planned to go there shortly for two weeks, I recommended that I go down there for one week with a married girlfriend of mine and the second week he could go down with his daughter. After those two weeks, I said, "Let's see how we feel when we get back – you without me and me without you." Deep down, I already knew my decision. Once I make up my mind about something, I just do it. My tragic flaw is that I make irrational decisions without thinking about the consequences. My father always said that I just jump into everything without thinking it through. Even to this day, he happens to be right. Why do smart women do stupid things? I don't know.

I went to Aruba. I spent an entire week sitting on the beach, talking with my girlfriend and trying to rationalize all of this, trying to think everything out. I always came up with the same thought. I didn't want to be married anymore. Did I want to be with Kamil? Absolutely! Did I have guilt over my marriage? Of course! Was it the freedom I desired so I could do what I wanted? Of course! I needed to be independent. I truly believed that since there were no children involved, no one would get hurt. My week in Aruba was over, and David and his daughter went down.

When he returned, we sat down in the den, and I said. "I want this to be a very friendly divorce." We both used the same lawyer. It was fourteen hundred dollars for the divorce, which David paid for. Three months later, our marriage was officially and legally over. It was quick; it was easy, no fault on either part. He owed my father some money, and the divorce settlement stipulated that he had to pay it back. Our suburban house was up for sale. David would live there until it was sold, and I was going to live in Manhattan. I was relieved and extremely excited.

Right after our decision to divorce, I went to work and told Kamil what I was doing. He was 100% behind me, but he did try to talk me out of it. He asked if I knew exactly what I was doing and if I really wanted to leave David and my marriage. I reassured him that I knew exactly what I was doing and that he, Kamil, had nothing to do with it. I told him that I desperately needed to be on my own. I said that our clandestine relationship had been going on for almost six years and I could no long continue the façade. I needed to get out of my loveless marriage – no matter what the consequences. He supported my decision. He responded that if this is what I really wanted to do and if there was nothing he could do to stop me, then so be it.

Kamil knew that I had always wanted to live in Manhattan. I had the 1986 Jaguar at the time, and it was brand new. I put an ad in the paper, and someone took over the lease since it made no sense to bring a car like that into Manhattan. Next, I went looking for apartments. I told David that the only furniture that I would take out of the house was the furniture I needed to live in Manhattan. I found my apartment in the city. It was a brand new building facing the river, a small one-bedroom apartment on the twenty-second floor. It was tiny, but it was home. I loved it! At least at the time, I thought I loved it, even though it was costing me $1,750 a month for a tiny box. I didn't care at that point. When I left David and moved to Manhattan, we had a dog, a husky. I left the dog at the house with David; this was the only difficult part of the divorce. After being in my new apartment for two months, I started to become extremely lonely. Of course, I was seeing Kamil at work and we were having dinner at least two or three nights a week, and seeing one another as much as we possible, but I was still lonely.

One Sunday, Kamil came into New York and said, " Come with me. I have a surprise for you." I excitedly said, "Where are we going?" He took me downtown to a pet store and bought me the cutest apricot poodle that you ever saw in your life. And Kamil named him, Poker. And that's how I got my beloved Poker. He was so cuddly and cute. He grew up to be the best dog in the world. When he was fourteen, he died in my arms. I was crying hysterically because I knew that he was the last thing I had in my life that was a living part of my lover – the love of my life. I remember calling Kamil to tell him that our child was gone. And I think he said something about its being just one of those things. That was in the year 2000. This affair had now been going on for many years. Like all relationships, it was fueled by love, passion, and friendship with all their highs and lows. But most fiery flames must die out.

Chapter Eighteen

FRIENDS, LOVERS NO MORE

Kamil and I shared a very unique relationship. Many books are written about such events. Our story might not seem unusual. What is unusual about this relationship is how long it went on even when we were no longer lovers. Also unusual is how our lives changed the moment we broke up in 1986. One evening, years later, as I was pondering our complex relationship, I switched on the television, and there was a show that was discussing death in the Middle East and the mourning process in that culture. It painfully brought me back to that devastating period when Kamil and I broke up. I always knew what it meant to lose someone you love dearly, but I never knew how deeply it affected me until this very moment, a moment of stark, agonizing realization.

That first week after we broke up, Kamil came into the store. He had grown a beard. I had just found out at that time that he was in mourning for forty days. He was mourning me and the death of our relationship. I didn't know it at that time, but not only did I have a mental breakdown after our breakup; Kamil did too. I never realized until that moment how deep and life-altering that mourning was for him. Maybe, for the first time after all these years, I finally understood what it meant when he said that we could never be together. Because after that forty-day mourning period, in his mind and heart, my soul left his and I was dead to him. Kamil mourned me for those forty days. After the mourning period for Middle Eastern men, that is the end. That was the end for us, at that point. And as I reflect back, I realize now why he was never the same after that. As much love as he had in his heart and soul for me, after the forty days, he released me. I mourned him also, but in my heart, I never let him go. Only in outward appearances did I let him go.

Chapter Nineteen
HEAVEN, I'M IN HEAVEN – OR HELL?

It is 1985, and I'm happily living in Manhattan. I'm comfortably settled in Manhattan with my beautiful dog, Poker, and Kamil and I are still devoted lovers. When I finally left David and was living in the city, I thought I had my own little heaven. I had the man I loved by my side, and I was foot loose and fancy free.

About six months prior, while I was still with David, Kamil decided to go into the manufacturing part of the jewelry business. He eventually moved to a new location. He became partners with another jeweler, and he asked me to stay at the jewelry salon and run that end of the business. At the time, a young man, named Jack was working for him as our runner, but Kamil was going to give him more responsible work. I told Kamil that if I was going to be running the jewelry store, I wanted Jack to be my partner. I would do the sales end of it, and Jack would do the inside work, and he agreed.

Kamil came to my house in the suburbs, and he, David, and I sat down at the kitchen table to discuss the financial arrangements. Kamil offered me $600 a week in cash, and I said I wanted Jack to

make the exact same amount of money. And that was the beginning of my special relationship with Jack as my partner and as my
life-long friend. At that time, Jack was not married. His wife,
Jill, would come into my life a little later on. Jack is a wonderful,
soft-spoken, person. We got along fantastically. So Kamil went
to his new company, and I worked with Jack.

When I finally left David and the house was sold, I received
my share of the sale of the house. Kamil needed money for his
new business. I never hesitated to offer it to him. I had $100,000
in the bank and offered the entire amount to him. Kamil, his
father, and I went to a Manhattan attorney. We sat down to
make an agreement for the payback of the money I gave him. I
never signed that agreement. I turned around and said to Kamil,
"I love you, and if you go under, I go down with you." With his
heavy accent, his honorable father said, "Don't worry; I'll make
sure that my son pays you back every single dollar." "Papa," I
responded, "Don't worry about it." I really wanted to give him
the money. He was the man I loved, and he needed it. It was
his dream! And I was going to help him make that dream come
true.

Kamil accepted the money with no interest or any strings attached. I told him that if I needed it, I would let him know. And
that is how his new company got started – his money, my money,
the bank's money, and everything that we could put together to
get this dream business of his started. It became very successful
very quickly. It did extremely well. He was making mountings,
he was opening up accounts, he was advertising, he was doing

a promotional book, and everything was working out magnificently. And Jack and I ran the jewelry store. It was running smoothly, and we were making a profit.

In 1985 and 1986, everything was going perfectly. We were like one big happy family. I was thrilled living in Manhattan, and Kamil's new business was becoming successful. Basically, I was really working for Kamil, the man I adored. I was ecstatic with my new unencumbered life.

Chapter Twenty

FOOLS RUSH IN

It's hard for me to pinpoint when things started to change, but it started rapidly – almost too rapidly. David had begun to date his girlfriend openly. He called me up one night and told me that he was going to marry her. I wished him luck, but I also asked him why he was rushing. I cautioned him that he was always hurrying into all these marriages. She was going to be his fifth wife. I told him to slow down and take a deep breath. But he didn't listen. He put himself into debt by taking all the money from the house, buying another condo, going to Europe, buying her a huge diamond ring, an expensive mink coat –spending more money than he had, like he had always done. He eventually got himself totally in debt. Look who is giving advice!

Meanwhile, I was working, paying my rent, going everywhere with Kamil whenever possible. I think we went to every hot spot in Manhattan from uptown to downtown and in between. At least once a week, we went to our favorite restaurant on the water; it became our special place. We loved sitting outside looking at the slow-moving water that gently relaxed and soothed us. Ironically and sadly, we were at our favorite spot when we broke up.

Chapter Twenty One
OUR HERNÁNDEZ'S HIDEAWAY

We all have moments that we remember as the best times of our lives, and I had mine in the early and middle '80s with Kamil before my divorce from David. People think that by having homes, cars, furs, and jewelry – that all those material things would make you happy, but the strangest part is that I spent the happiest time of my life in a 12- by 16-foot studio apartment in Lower Manhattan that was owned by Kamil and his best pal. It became our romantic hideaway. Original, the place was unsightly. There was an elderly man who resided there; I believe it was someone Kamil knew from the "Old Country." We went there one day, and the place was infested with cockroaches. It was dirty, filthy, dark, and disgusting. Kamil gave the old gent two thousand dollars; he instructed him to go to the YMCA and told him he had to move. Kamil gave him a week to do so. We went back to the place, threw everything out, and fumigated it.

Kamil gave me twenty thousand dollars, and I put my decorating skills to good use. I turned that undistinguished 12- by 16-foot little hole-in-the-wall on the second floor in the city

– probably a place that no one would even entertain the thought of looking at never mind living in – into a dynamite, gorgeous space. But I loved it because it belonged to Kamil and me. I put in forest green carpets and painted the walls an equally rich forest green. There was a double window over the radiator that faced the brick wall of the building across the way. No view whatsoever. I had custom shades made in a soft silvery gray with a pattern that had the shade of the hunter green in the carpet and walls and accented it with lavender. To compliment it, I had a hide-a-way bed covered in the same fabric. In front of it, I placed a brass and glass cocktail table. Flower arrangements were placed strategically in the right corner; a standing lamp was placed on the other side to give a soft glow to the room. There was a minute alcove that could be used for a Murphy bed, and I put a TV in a shelf wall unit in that space. On the radiator, I placed a beautiful, exotic Egyptian head on one of the shelves by the TV, and I put a brass naked woman with her hands seductively above her head, which Kamil loved because he said it looked like me. Also in that apartment, because he loved Elvis Presley, we put the look-alike doll and the life-like painting of Elvis. There was a mirror above the sofa and, as you entered the apartment, we had a brass mini-bar with a small refrigerator. We re-glazed the entire bathroom and had all the fixtures replaced in ivory; we accessorized with hunter green towels. I loved that Kamil trusted and believed in me to transform this remote, disarrayed place into a homing nest. This transformed space became our secret love nest. No more hotels, no more obscure motels and spots to hide in. This was our place!

Kamil had bought this studio many years ago with his best friend and cohort, Lorenzo. Maria, Kamil's wife, didn't know it still existed. She was under the erroneous assumption that when they got married, he had sold it. So it became our home, not only for lovemaking but also for relaxing, conversing, and sharing our inner most feelings, especially when things of uncertainty were happening to us. Similar to a Woody Allen setting, we had many happy times just sitting on the floor, eating Chinese right out of the cartons, watching TV, and frequently just doing nothing. I adored this place. This little 12 by 16 "hole-in-the-wall" was my salvation. I stayed over night many times when David was out of town, and I didn't want to go back to New Jersey. It was my home away from home. Kamil loved it too. When we broke up, he told me to go in there and take out anything I wanted because, he said, he would never go back into that place for the rest of his life.

It wasn't until the late '90s that I saw Kamil again after a number of years. I had gone back to New Jersey to visit my girlfriend, and he and I reconnected. He picked me up at my girlfriend's house, and we drove alone together to his summer home on Long Island. It was one of the last times that Kamil and I were physically and sexually together. When I walked into the house, there were two things in there that stunned me. One was the exotic Egyptian head on his mantle over his fireplace and the other was the brass naked/erotic woman placed in full view on a table. Here it was ten years later, and he still had those pieces. He obviously did go back to that apartment. He took out the Elvis Hirschfield sketching I had given to him many years earlier; it now hung in his summer home. He also had the Elvis doll. I assumed that these personal items represented me. I knew then that Kamil had never totally separated from me emotionally – only physically. Years after we had broken up, he kept those precious items that I have given him; not the leather luggage, the fur coat, or any of the material things – rather the meaningful ones. That insignificant head and statue symbolized our life together and our enduring love.

Over the years, even after we had broken up, he continued sending me gifts at Christmas. I still have some beautiful things that he gave me. Time marches on, but I treasure and admire the beautiful Cartier desk clock that he gave me when I had my apartment in the upper eastside of New York. Kamil had a fetish for Cartier. He bought me beautiful wine goblets from there; he also gave me a gorgeous heavy black obelisk when I moved to my New Jersey house that I still keep in my current place on my armoire. I still have many elegant frames from Tiffany and Cartier's, gifts that he sent me when I was living in California only four years ago. When I was working there in the jewelry business, he sent me a beautiful glass frame in which I have a photo of my two precious dogs, my beloved Poker and my adorable BoBo.

Chapter Twenty Two

WORDS AND ACTIONS TO REGRET:
LOVE ME, LOVE ME NOT

Ironically, we separated in 1986, and he is still showering me with memorable gifts. Isn't that strange? Indicating that some way, some how, we are still very much connected. It is an amazing story about what I had to go through to survive after we broke up. I ended the relationship with Kamil; he did not break up with me. And that is the strangest part of this story. The night I told him to leave my apartment in New York City, he cautioned me that if he walked out the door, he would never be back. And, of course, with my hasty attitude, I irresponsibly responded, "Fine! Don't come back." I simply didn't think of the possible long-term ramifications and life-altering implications of those simple words. Little did I know that those words would come back to haunt me my entire life. Little did I know that those few words would put me in therapy, would make me want to commit suicide, would put me in a financial bind. To this very day, those four words, uttered without thought, permanently changed my life. Those stupid little words that every woman has said to every man in her life at one point or another: "Get out. I don't care if I ever see you again." It has been said so many times before that when men and women are having affairs, most of the time it works because there is no pressure. While I was married and Kamil was married, there was no undue pressure. Kamil never had to worry what I was doing after the fact because he knew I was going home to someone – someone who was there to take care of me when he could not. I, in turn, knowing how he felt about his wife, Maria, didn't care that he was going home. I envied her that she was sleeping with him every night, but I also had my husband on the other end. So all the years that we were together, there was no added pressure on his part. Kamil didn't have to worry that if there was a holiday and he couldn't be with me, I wouldn't be alone. All that changed when David and I got divorced and I was living alone in Manhattan. Of course, I was still working at the jewelry salon – everything in that department was fine. But then all of a sudden, little things started to change. One time, Kamil and I were sitting at our favorite café having a conversation, and he said to me, "I think maybe you should keep busy because I can't see you all the time; maybe you should start dating." I immediately said, "Are you crazy? Why would you want me to go out with anyone else?" He responded, "Not anything serious, just casual, just to keep you company in case I can't see you on a Saturday night." I said, "Fine, if that's what you want." The more he pushed me, the more I gave in. I didn't like what I was hearing, and I knew I wasn't going to go out of my way to meet anyone. Occasionally an opportunity to date someone else fell into my lap, and that happened one night when I met a man in a restaurant. This person asked me out; he wanted me to see the Neil Diamond concert with him. The irony of this was, I wasn't aware that Kamil had already bought tickets for the same show for us to see together. Unaware, I made arrangements with this man to go to the concert. After that, I was having a drink with Kamil at our special restaurant on the Hudson River, and I told him about my date. I was determined not to keep anything from him. I said that I had met this man, that it was no big deal, and that he had bought tickets for us to see Neil Diamond. Immediately, and with anger, Kamil pulled out of his pocket two, two hundred dollar tickets that he had purchased to take me to see the same show. I said, "Oh, my God, I didn't know you were going to get tickets." He reminded me that I had told him that I wanted to see Neil Diamond, so he had gone out and bought tickets. He shouted, "Now you are going to see it with someone else"? He took the two tickets and ripped them in half and threw them in the river. I said, "What are you doing?" He angrily shouted, "You don't need me to take you to see Neil Diamond. You already have a date." I screamed back, "I thought this is what you wanted? Why are you arguing with me?" And that was the beginning of the breakdown of our incredible relationship. The fighting began and became more frequent. Something we had never done. A declining relationship is a painful experience, but a failing clandestine love relationship is unbearable. You have no legal rights or claim on the person.

Many things lead up to this decline. I became frequently upset and concerned about his drinking, yet I tried not to pressure him too much about it because he got that from his wife. Did I like it? No! There was even a time when I had my brand new Burgundy two-seater sports Jaguar car and we went to this top-notch restaurant for dinner and he drank through the entire meal. He did this no matter where we went. After we had dinner, we got in my car, and I was driving him home. Looking sallow and groggy, he turned to me and said, "I feel sick." Concerned, I asked, "What's the matter?" He said, "I'm going to throw up." I told him to put his head out of the car. Mind you, my car was less than a week old; my husband had just bought it for me, and I loved it. Kamil had the identical model, but a different color. He threw up, not only out the window, but also all over my new car. How was I going to explain that to my husband? I decided to take him back to our studio apartment instead of his house. I held his head over the toilet, I cleaned him up, and when I knew he was OK, I went back to New Jersey. This incident was just one of the many times I held his head over a toilet. Of course, I told my husband that I was the one who got sick; I took the blame. When you're deeply in love and deeply committed, you do strange and daring things. Navigating two relationships became very complex. Ambiguous feelings fuel your guilt, but something else keeps you from heeding the obvious warnings. Kamil's and my relation was unraveling. Yet there were so many good times, and I was trying to recall them to try and recapture those old feelings again. One that vividly stands out in my mind was his thirty-fifth birthday. I wanted to give him a fabulous surprise. I bought him the watch that he had lost a few years later. The day of his birthday, I had a limo come to the jewelry store to pick us up. I rented a suite in an opulent hotel in the heart of our beloved city. Lorenzo and his girlfriend were going to meet us there for a celebratory champagne and steak dinner. There were lively and colorful balloons strewn around the suite, the chilled champagne was flowing freely, and I was paying for the entire event. I remember how excited he was when I presented him with the watch. But lately, there seemed to be more unfortunate incidents than good ones.

The night of the party, I was watching with baited breath for him to come to the jewelry shop so we could get in the limo and go to the hotel. Here it was, 7 p.m., and no Kamil. Lorenzo tried to locate him but to no avail. I was out of my mind and full of rage. Finally, at 7:30 he saunters in. He was pie-eyed. I angrily asked him "Where the hell were you?' He shot back, "What the hell does it matter? It's my birthday, so I was out drinking." Since it was, I ignored it. We got into the limo, and he started to kiss me and told me how sorry he was. He was like a little child full of excitement celebrating his birthday. We got to the hotel; the suite was magnificent; we ate, drank, and had loads of fun. Basically, we were having an orgy. Lorenzo and his gal were screwing in the other room, and Kamil and I were at it on the couch, on the floor, and in the bed. We stayed there until all hours into the night; but it had to end. I had to get home since I was still married. But it was well worth it, especially when I saw the look on Kamil's face and the tears in his eyes when I gave him the watch. That look of love and gratitude he gave me I will never forget.

Another time that I will always remember was in our studio apartment on my birthday, which is Valentine's Day. Lorenzo and his girlfriend were also there. I went there before I went to meet my husband for dinner. I looked exceptionally gorgeous that night in my brown silk dress. When I got there, Lorenzo and his gal gave us matching flannel nightgowns with little hearts strewn all over them. Kamil's had the blue hearts and mine had the red hearts. We took pictures of us in them; we absolutely adored them. Here we were, celebrating my birthday in that little apartment, having drinks, receiving whimsical gifts, just having fun – and then I had to leave to go be with my husband. It didn't matter that I did this behind my husband's back because I was so mesmerized, consumed, and deeply in love with Kamil, and I believe it was mutual. One time, Kamil bought tickets for himself and his wife to see Diana Ross, a show that I desperately wanted to see. He recognized my disappointment, so he went out and bought two more tickets to take David and me the following night. At times, the four of us went to shows together, Kamil and his wife, and David and me. Kamil sat next to his wife, I was on his other side, and my husband sat next to me. There I was, sitting in the middle between my lover and my husband, and I was as happy as could be.

Chapter Twenty Three

THE ROARING/DISRUPTIVE 80S: OLD MEMORIES, NEW BEGINNINGS

There wasn't anything that made me unhappy – the '80s were great! I was beautiful; I was in my forties; I was in the prime of my life; I had a handsome husband; I had fabulous friends; I had my parents, I belonged to a country club; I had a lovely home; I had luxury cars, furs, and jewelry; but, most important, I had and was deeply in love with the man who was my whole life, Kamil. Yet, I was blinded to all his faults. No matter what he did, I forgave him. No matter what he said, I forgave him. No matter how much he hurt me, I forgave him. I never let him know when he hurt me or when he got me angry. Personally, I believe I felt sorry for him because he had such an unhappy relationship with his wife. Actually, I know I felt sorry for him more than I did for myself. They say love is blind; well, I was blind as a bat! To me, it was a wonderful, exciting loving relationship but a very strange one, too, with all its harrowing twists and turns, highs and lows, and emotional ups and downs. I accepted all of his faults because, when I reflect back, Kamil truly never let me down, perhaps because he felt extremely guilty over the fact that I divorced my husband. Even to this day, he feels he is responsible. I have always reassured him that I mostly likely would have eventually divorced David. But, to be totally truthful, if I had never met Kamil, I most likely would never have divorced my husband. As fate would have it, David died very young, so I would have been alone anyway. After David died, it made it a little easier for Kamil to cope with his guilt and absolve himself from his feelings of betrayal.

Kamil, after we broke up and after his mourning period, emotionally closed down, and I did too. The first week after we broke up, I was in control. I walked with my head held high. When I came into the jewelry store, I acted as if nothing was wrong. My outward attitude was flippant; I said, "Screw you!" "Who cares?" But then the days and nights started to pass, and the unbearable loneliness set in. At that point, in 1987, I bought a one-bedroom apartment in New York. You see, Kamil paid me back the $100,000 he had borrowed from me, and he also gave me some money to live off since I had stopped working at the jewelry store. That's when I went for my real estate license. I desperately tried to keep myself active and busy. I bought beautiful new furniture, and I decided to make a life without him. It was the beginning of another era of my life. So I thought! This should be easy, having my own apartment in New York, starting to date, life without Kamil, and no more jewelry store. I thought living in Manhattan would be easy for me, even knowing that he would not be far from me. I tried to convince my self,

"Who cares about the jewelry store where he is, who cares about the apartment which was our love nest, who cares that he is still married to his wife, and I'm going to get through all this. I'm a survivor." So I thought!

I was in therapy twice a week, which Kamil paid for. When I went to my therapist's office, I walked in with my head held high in my mink coat and sexy boots. I was play-acting. This all occurred because, two months after we broke up, I couldn't function. I wasn't going out. I would lie in bed all night just staring at the ceiling, night after night after night. I was smoking two packs of cigarettes a day – I, who hardly ever smoked. I was like *Valley of the Dolls*; I took Valium at night to sleep. I tried to keep busy in the apartment to keep my mind occupied, but my mind was not cooperating – it was frantic at times and cold and blank other times. I couldn't read, I couldn't watch TV and I couldn't do anything. I was a non-functioning zombie. I completely shut down. That's when I recognized that I was in desperate need of help. But whom was I going to turn to? I was divorced from my husband, my father was gone, I couldn't talk to my mother, my sister and I had no relationship, my friends thought I was crazy to begin with and they were trying to be as supportive as possible. My only alternative, so I thought, was to go to Kamil. I told him I needed therapy but couldn't afford it. I begged him to go with me; telling him that maybe we'd get through this together. "No," he said, "I don't believe in therapy. You go, I'll pay for it." My friend recommended this therapist. She had gone to him years back, and even had slept with him. Guess the old adage that therapists need therapy has some merit, but he was brilliant. He had written many scholarly texts. At the onset of my therapy, he hypnotized me and gave me a stress test. I hit nine and a half – and ten was the highest. That's how stressed out I was the first year after we'd broken up. I totally broke down.

Chapter Twenty Four

STRANGERS IN THE NIGHT

Since I couldn't make it in real estate, I needed a job. Unable to concentrate, I never even completed the classes. Kamil gave me a job in the jewelry store and reassured me that I would always have a job. Once again, he was in my life, and we weren't even going together. So, in 1987 I went back into the jewelry store and worked with Jack. I felt at home there, I felt a connection, so I began to feel somewhat better. Looking back, I think it was the worst thing I could have done because periodically Kamil stopped into the store unannounced. I saw him on the street, or I saw him where he worked when I had to go pick up something. The first few months, we didn't even look at each other, let alone speak. Not even a word. Eventually we got to the point where we could talk to each other and at times even went out to lunch. We tried to talk things through, but it was obvious that we were never going to get back together again. The first years, we did not sleep with each other. We were afraid. Where we afraid of getting back to that uncontrollable and dangerous passion? When he inquired as to how I was doing, I pretended that things were better, especially since therapy. Actually, of course, they were not.

In 1987, I had a terrible scare; I found a suspicious lump in my breast – every woman's nightmare. Needless to say, I was petrified. I didn't even tell my mother. My doctor told me he would put me into the hospital as an outpatient to do a biopsy. I told Kamil. For some reason, I wanted him to know, I believe because I feared something might happen to me. My girlfriend came into New York and picked me up at the hospital after the biopsy, brought me home, and took care of me. Thank God it was benign. But it was a terrible scare, and I related this to Kamil, and as always, he was very concerned and caring. I felt as if he was my best friend. For some reason, everything that happened in my life – men, moving, financial difficulties, illness, and death – he was always involved in. I made him a part of my life. I made him *my* life. Of course, in therapy, they advise you that you have to let go and move on with your life. You have to forget they stress, and they tell you to pack up all the things that are associated with him and remove them from your life. They suggested that I make a collage of my life, which I painstakingly did. In the middle of my collage, I put a golden coach. I had birds, cars, and clothes from *Vogue* and other material items in it. For me, the birds symbolized how I was always in flight and how I could never stay put for a long period of time. Which is very true. It was still true even later in life when I flittered around like a gypsy. Reflecting back, I recognize that I had never had roots. I didn't care that I owned things because I felt they were replaceable and that I could leave everything behind. When I moved, I thought I had left all behind. I never carried my personal baggage with me – at least that is what I assumed. This is my M.O. Most people save things for a lifetime – in a box such as letters, sentimental items, that sort of thing. I saved nothing. It was as if the past never existed for me; it was something I wanted to forget.

We all have good memories of our past that we dwell on, and we desperately try to forget the bad ones. So what was I doing? I was bringing my past into my future. I refused to let go. My psychiatrist would warn me, "You see the way you are now, fifty-years old and a good-looking woman? Do you want to still be good looking at fifty-five or sixty? If you continue the way you are going, you will surely burn out. You will never be able to have a serious relationship or stability in your life because you won't let go of the past." Now I am sixty-four and, sadly, I realize that he was absolutely right. I never let go, making it impossible for me to better my future. Fear of commitment and fear of other men paralyzed me. I sabotaged my security, my ability to love again, and my ability to trust again. I found fault with every new man that came into my life because I compared them to Kamil because I didn't want anyone but Kamil. And the tragedy is that he was and never will be perfect. After such a blatant betrayal, your self-esteem shrivels. You begin to question your own judgment. As I share this cautionary tale, I have become keenly aware that I made him into something unique and special, and he wasn't! He was and is just an ordinary person. He might have been exceptionally good-looking, extremely caring, and very exciting, but, in retrospect, he was just an ordinary guy with multiple faults. Kamil was interested only in himself; he was self-centered and ego driven. He believed that he had a sense of entitlement. Kamil was a man operating without a conscience or a moral compass. I guess we were similar; but I always put him first. I excused him because he kept his innermost feelings and his personal life to himself. He would never reveal anything about himself to anyone. The bottom line was that he always did what was best for him. Unfortunately, I was blind to this fact and I didn't know it until much later in life – until too late, in fact.

So here I am, in therapy, alone, and back working in the jewelry salon. Kamil is still married, and my life is unraveling slowly but surely. On top of all this, I have to deal with Kamil's wife since she is working at the jewelry salon and desperately wants me out of there. Her ultimatum to her husband was, "She is out, or I leave you and take the children with me to Europe to be with my family and we will never come back." Strange as it might seem, Kamil stood up for me. He adamantly refused to succumb to her threats. He reiterated that I was his friend, that I needed a job, and that I was a woman alone and divorced, and he emphatically stated that she had no right to tell him what to do. Is that the way he expressed his love for me – by standing up for me and refusing to succumb to his wife's demands? I wanted desperately to believe this. To be honest, I was surprised. Things settled down for a few months, but eventually it resurfaced. She wanted me out of there, and she was relentless in her pursuit, making me surmise that she knew about Kamil and me. Actually, I believe that she had always known. In fact, there was one time when Kamil and I were in a restaurant and when we left and was out front, he passionately kissed me. I looked up and his wife was walking down the street toward us. I believe she saw us, but she acted as if nothing happened. But as Kamil told me from the very beginning, "Deny, deny, deny." Then one day, it finally happened. He came to me and said that he had no choice, "My wife wants you out. She's threatening me, and as much as I have a strong hold on her, I don't want anything to disrupt my children." Realizing his dilemma and still being deeply in love with him, I told him that I would leave. I reassured him that I had no intention of making any trouble for him with his wife and his children because I knew how much his children meant to him. I said to him that I loved him enough to sacrifice everything so he wouldn't have to deal with her. Now I see that I never fought for myself because I never wanted to deny him his happiness, even at my own expense. It is human to long for love, to want to shower it and receive it, but not when it is damaging and destructive.

This need to keep him happy dissipated when, approximately six months after we broke up and I was working in the jewelry business, I had to go over to Kamil's office to deliver something. When I walked in, he got extremely angry that I had shown up instead of sending someone else. For the very first time ever, he rushed over to me, roughly took my arm, and pushed me out of the office while screaming at the top of his lungs that he never wanted me to set foot in his office again. He caused such a commotion that his father came into the office and couldn't believe what was going on. I actually went home that night with my arm black and blue. I was shocked and stunned by his behavior since he had never raised his hand to me, pushed, or shoved me nor has he ever used physical force on me before. But I should have known better because his father had used physical force on Kamil's wife after a huge fight; he actually punched her in the face. Why do some women make excuses for physical abuse by men? Age-old question.

I had a new apartment in Upper Manhattan for almost two years. At this time, it is around 1989, and I was very unhappy in New York. I was lonely and still longing for what was. I wasn't working at the jewelry salon any longer. I was working at various jewelry stores. Nothing made me happy. Manhattan no longer made me happy because I couldn't be at the places where Kamil was. So I decided to leave. I put the apartment up for sale and made a hundred thousand dollars when it was sold. Thankfully, the market was still strong in New York at that time. But what to do now? I asked myself. "Where will I go?" I decided to go back to where I came from, New Jersey. I moved to Edgewater and took a one-bedroom apartment. The problem was that when I sat out by the pool, I could view Manhattan. This upset me. I didn't want to see Manhattan, and I didn't even want to look over there. Everything in Manhattan reminded me of Kamil. Every inch of Manhattan reminded me of him because at one time or another we were in every inch of Manhattan from downtown to midtown to uptown. From across town to Long Island – all the way to New Jersey. Even in New Jersey, every place I went reminded me of a time when I had been there with Kamil. Archers Restaurant, the Bicycle Club, and the seedy little motels we frequented on Route 4. After awhile, I couldn't handle it. Even, my ex-husband and his new wife were living ten minutes from me. To add to this, I was working for a friend of Kamil's, a jeweler in Ft. Lee. I was trying to have a life independent of Kamil but it wasn't working. You see, I was still talking with him on the phone and periodically seeing him socially but not sexually. Like my psychiatrist said, I wasn't letting go. I still forgave all that he had done to me and continued to long for him.

Then one day in July of 1989, something happened that shook me to the core. I received a phone call from a friend with terrible news. My former husband, David, had died suddenly. At first I didn't believe her. I was shocked; I couldn't believe it. Here was a man that I had been with for seventeen years – and married to for fourteen of those years. He was only fifty-six years old, in the prime of his life, and now he was gone forever just like that. Ironically, I had seen him about a week before at the movies with his new wife. We just casually said hello. In retrospect, he didn't look well. He was still gorgeous, but he didn't seem happy. I found out later that a few months prior, he had had a minor heart attack. Strange thing was that he lost his father of a heart attack at the age of fifty-nine, also in the month of July. Needing to find some comfort, I once again turned to Kamil. He was also shocked and in disbelief. We met in New York for lunch, we talked things over, and we talked about David and our life together.

Feeling compelled to do something for David, I offered one of my family plots to his current wife for his burial, but she, not being Jewish, refused it. So David was placed in another cemetery where no one else he knew was buried. I felt that he was all alone. Little did he know that I was just as alone – and I'm not even dead! The night before the funeral, I called David's only daughter to tell her about her father. She didn't want to go since they had been alienated from one another for a few years. Sadly, David didn't even know that she was married and had a child – his grandchild. The following morning, she had a change of heart and called to say that she would be attending with her mother. I also contacted all our friends to tell them that David was gone. Some came and some didn't. The day of the services was a dismal, raining day. The rain poured down hard and fast, like the tears streaming down my face. When I walked into the funeral home that morning by myself, my former sister-in-law and my former mother-in-law were standing there. My mother-in-law came up to me and said, "You killed him." I will never forget that. This was a funeral that should have been in every paper in the country because there has never been anything like it that I can recall. For example, David's daughter was sitting in the limo crying. Friends of mine came over to me to tell me that David's wife would not allow David's daughter to view her father. Before I knew it, the police were at the door. They came to me and wanted to escort me out of the funeral home. I couldn't believe what was going on in a house of worship – police asking people to leave and a bereaved daughter crying in a limo. I warned the police to keep their hands off of me and told them I would leave of my own accord. I got into the limo with David's daughter and her mother, and she told me that his wife wouldn't let her view her father and that she just wanted to leave a picture of her baby, his grandchild, with him. The three rejected members of David's family left and went to have lunch in Fort Lee. I promised David's daughter that I would take her to the cemetery to visit with her father at a later date. For some reason, it never materialized. I never took her, and I have no knowledge as to whether she ever went, but I went, about a year later. I sat at his gravesite and cried my eyes out. I cried my eyes out asking him for forgiveness, I cried my eyes out for him because he was gone, I cried my eyes out because of what I had done to the relationship. I wanted his forgiveness. But it was too late.

His daughter and I kept in touch for a while after that. It didn't work because she had a husband, a child, a mother and a stepfather, step sisters and brothers, and I was an outsider. The last time I saw her was just before I moved to Florida in 1990. And to this day, I have never seen nor heard from her or anyone from David's family.

Chapter Twenty Five

A CHANGE OF SCENERY

Up until about two years ago, Kamil would ask me if I felt guilty about David. I believe he was questioning me because he was experiencing guilt for everything that happened to me over the next ten years: without David, without him, and my having to survive on my own. When David died, I knew that I had to leave the area. My father was gone, and my mother had been living in Boca Raton, Florida, since 1984. In 1988, I decided to go down there to visit my mother. She wanted me to move to Florida; I didn't know what I wanted to do. But I knew I had to do something because I was losing my mind. I was living in Edgewater, NJ, I was working in a small jewelry store, and I was totally miserable. I thought it was time for me to get away from all of it. I never wanted to see Kamil again, I never wanted to hear his name again, I no longer wanted to be involved with him, I didn't want to dream about him or think about him, so I looked in Florida for a place to live. I had put the money made from the sale of the apartment in Manhattan into the stock market, and Kamil had given me a substantial amount of money when

I left the jewelry salon. So financially, I was fine. I wound up buying a villa in Boca Raton, which was then just being built. It was to be completed in about one year. To be honest with you, it was my dream home. In 1990, I paid close to two hundred thousands dollars for it, which was a lot of money. It looked absolutely magnificent after I decorated it. It was a new start for me. I began to sell jewelry in Florida from a suitcase, making about five thousand dollars a month. I was getting it from all my old sources in New York, even from Kamil. Hence, he was still in my life, and even moving to Florida didn't distance me from him emotionally. When I would get depressed, I would call him. I made all sorts of excuses just to contact him – my business, my mother, my loneliness. I even discussed with him the guys I was dating. It was an unsettling time for me. Even though I had moved away physically, I was still attached to him. So moving to another state, having a new home, making new friends, becoming close to a family down there – none of it made a difference when it came to my feelings for Kamil. At first I thought disengaging from him was the solution, but deep down inside, I know it wasn't.

When I moved to Florida, I dated, and I became sexually involved with a variety of diverse men, a Frenchman, an Israeli, an Italian waiter. Anyone who would show me the smallest amount of attention I would sleep with. I tried anything just to get Kamil out of my head. I was in constant search of another man, a man of my dreams, a man to replace Kamil. But, of course, that didn't happen. Friends frequently fixed me up but to no avail. Every time I slept with someone else, I would think about and even compare them to Kamil. Then I would cry because, for some reason, I felt as if I were cheating on him. The depression after we broke up was unbearable. Even therapy didn't seem to help. Looking back, I can recognize that it did help, but at the time, I was vulnerable, raw, and not willing to accept the reality of what is. I resisted any advice given to me. All I wanted was to have my relationship back with Kamil the way it had been earlier on. Nothing I did worked. Sooner or later, you learn that while you can run away, everything eventually follows you. There are some things that you can't shut off, and they are your mind and heart. Of course, you can block things out, but they will come back to haunt you. You can just push so much down inside for so long, and then it will come out in distorted ways. Clearly, I was possessed.

Did I think that God was punishing me? Absolutely! I just couldn't get my life together. I needed and desired Kamil for every little thing. We decided that it would be best for us to be friends. Did I still love him? Yes. But I decided I would have to learn to love him as a friend because I needed him in my life. He was like my salvation, he was my answer to everything, and he was my excuse for everything. When I was unhappy, I blamed him; if I was happy, it was because of him; if I was financially poor, he helped me. Even when I had money, I never paid him back, I knew I didn't have to – he never asked for one damn penny back. He never expected it. But I think that was also part of his guilt. Perhaps he thought it was a payoff. Giving to me would absolve him of his guilt. To this day, I believe he suffers deep guilt, as I do, for all the people around us who were hurt because of our selfish indiscretions.

Moving to Florida was clearly not an answer. It was just a different location. As I mentioned earlier, I had other relationships in Florida. I even got engaged. Obviously that didn't work out. I threw him out. Again, I never wanted to fully commit to anyone after Kamil. I thought I did, and I tried, I really tried. I was frantically searching, hanging out at bars with other lonely single people my age. It was what I thought would alleviate my loneliness and pain. Actually, the first year I was without Kamil, 1989, wasn't too bad. I was coping. I was even somewhat happy. I had a beautiful home. I was making some money and having some income come in from my investments. My mother was well. I had some family in Florida, and many friends came down to visit me from New York – the snowbirds. I developed some relationships, all assisting me to block out the memories of my life in New York with Kamil. Yet, with all this, I still could not get him out of my head or heart. I had to see him. I was in Florida a year, and I felt compelled to see him. So I called him and told him that I was coming to New York and thought it would be nice to see him for old time's sake. I used the excuse that I was coming up to purchase some jewelry at the show. He responded, "Sure, let's go out for a drink."

I met him in New York at the jewelry show, and I will never forget that moment when my eyes met his. I completely melted. It was five years since we had broken up, and I realized that nothing had changed – every part of my body craved him, desired him, and longed for him. The pain of love only increased my rapture for him. For me the pain of love for him was being alive again. Yet, I continued to play the role of *friend* because I didn't want him to get the best of me. I didn't want to give in; I didn't want my wall of protection to break and flood me with more passion and emotions. We left the show and went out for a couple of drinks at Rockefeller Center, which we used to frequent. He looked at me and I looked at him, and we wound up in a room in a hotel. We made mad, passionate love, and it was exactly as before. All those years of separation just melted away. It was as if we were starting all over again. The only difference was that he was still in New York and I was in Florida. I knew then that I would never get over him. I didn't know what to do. I returned to Florida; I went back to work. Occasionally I sent him a card, never forgetting his birthday, and never forgetting him on Christmas or Father's Day. Any little thing that I could do, I did for him from the heart. He was my everything!

Chapter Twenty Six

JOURNEYING AND REMEMBERING

There are so many things that you think and remember about a relationship, especially when looking back upon it. One of things that I remember the most are the short trips I took with Kamil in the happy times of our relationship. I think those were the happiest times I ever had in any relationship and at any other point in my life. The first one was in the Hamptons – West Hampton. Kamil's wife was away at their beach house. Kamil asked me to get a room at a local hotel in the Hamptons; he would meet me there. So I told my husband that I was going to the Hamptons with my girlfriends just for the weekend since he wasn't even going to be home. I had taken a small cabin away from the main area of the hotel. It was very private. I checked in, and I anxiously waited for his arrival. Kamil called me from the road, telling me that he was going to be late, which, as I mentioned before, was nothing unusual for him. I gave him the cabin number. Little did I know that he was standing at the front door when I arrived there. We were both dressed casually, so we went in and changed our clothes to something more substantial and went out to dinner. It was as if we were married. We acted like a married couple going on a mini vacation. Unfortunately, our little fantasy vacation had to be cut short since he had to leave the next day to go back to New York to the jewelry store. After he left, I went to the pool overlooking the ocean, and I'll never forget that the theme song from *Chariots of Fire* was playing on the tape that I had just purchased. Every time I hear that song, it reminds me of that fabulous weekend I spent in the Hamptons with the love of my life. When he left, Kamil left his dirty clothes and socks, so, like a dutiful wife, I washed them and laid them on the bushes outside the cabin to dry. It was almost like being at camp. I adored doing things like that for him. He came back earlier that evening; I couldn't wait to see him. My heart pounded whenever I thought about or saw him. When he returned, we made love, went out to dinner, took long leisurely walks on the beach, and watched the seagulls fly over our heads while the ocean waves ebbed and flowed in and out like my fluttering heart. We swam in the pool, never letting each other go – we were each other's life preservers. Oh, the romantic things you do with someone when you are deeply in love. It was such a magnificent time.

I fondly recall another time when we went down to the Jersey shore. I made another frequently used excuse to David: I needed to get away for a few days. I checked into a spa. Kamil came to meet me at night; we spent the night making love and then under the radiant moonlight, holding hands, walking along the beach watching the dazzling stars glitter above us. It was such an enchanting private time. We were deliriously in love and all alone. No one knew where we were or what we were doing.

I remember still another time. It was in an unusually warm October, and David had gone out of town for a day or two. Kamil and I decided to go to Washington, DC. It was the last time I would see him before that February when we broke up. We checked into a fabulous Five-Star hotel in DC. The room was gorgeous. We ordered room service, and after that, we made wild passionate love. I had brought winter clothes with me, but it was close to ninety degrees out. The first night, we ate at a seafood restaurant on the water and drove around the city; then we walked arm in arm as the lights of DC illuminated brightly. Washington, DC, is gorgeous, especially when you are in love. The following day, we purchased tickets for the show *Argentine Tango* – featuring lots of fabulous sexy dancing. It was incredible. We went to dinner that night, and I was dressed in a winter skirt, heavy sweater, and stockings. I was beastly hot. I kept complaining to Kamil about how hot I felt. He sneaked under the table and slowly, gently, and erotically pulled my stockings off. These are some of the wonderful, crazy things he used to do that made our relationship fun, spontaneous, and exciting, and I savored every single one of them. We would go back to the hotel, we'd lie in bed, and the outside world melted away. It was if we were the only two people left in the world. After love-making, he would encase me in his arms, and I was filled with so much love for him. In his strong safe arms, I knew that I wanted him in my life for the rest of my life. He was my spiritual husband, my friend, my lover, and my confidant. I trusted him, and I respected him. Besides his being gorgeous, sexy, spontaneous, and fun, he was everything I could ever want in man. But the reality was that I wasn't married to him. He was someone else's husband. I knew that I was living on the edge. I didn't want that weekend to end. These were some of the greatest moments of my life with him. Times we shared away from everything and everybody. Nobody was watching us, nobody was telling us what to do, no work, just us. It was an incredible time to reflect, to talk, to make love, to be together, and with not a care in the world. People dream of going to Europe and exotic places, and here we were close to home having a wonderful time.

The only other time that I would be alone with him would be many years later in the '90s, after we had broken up. He came down to Florida to see me. I was living in North Miami. I had my second poodle, BoBo, at that time, and he came to stay with me. That was wonderful too. Here it was so many years later, and we weren't together, yet we were together. He slept at my place, we made love, we went to Bal Harbor, we walked to various places, we ate cozy dinners in outside cafes, we went down to Miami, to South Beach and visited the chic Delano Hotel. We sat in the back of the beach at the famous Delano, talked, and went over our past lives. At this time, he was already divorced from his wife, so he had more freedom. I, of course, was divorced, and David was deceased. Neither one of us had any relationships to interfere, but strangely enough, we didn't get back together. There were many times as the years would pass when I would see him. But that was the last time we actually had sleepovers. That was in 1997, before I moved to Arizona.

Chapter Twenty Seven
TWIST AND TURNS

As I said earlier, there are many twists and turns to this story. This is a story about a relationship that went on for years and years, a relationship in which Kamil was always in my heart and, I truly believe, I was in his heart. Was I wishing that we would get back together? Yes! Did I want to marry him? Yes! Did I try to talk myself out of it? Yes! Because I knew he would go back to New York, back to his old life, back to his children, to his girl-friend, whom I think he had met many, many years ago. Kamil had known her since she was a young girl coming into the jewelry store with her mother. She married and got divorced. Evidently they would get together now and then even when I was in his life, but I never knew it. Actually, when he came down to Florida to see me, he also saw her. He also went to see my mother, who was in an assistant living care facility. Whenever he came to see her, he made my mother so happy. I didn't know whether it was be-cause she knew how much I loved him or because of the goodness that he had shown her over the years. I remember her saying to him, "Please take care of my daughter. Don't ever let her down."

She made him promise. And he tried to keep his promise. For whatever reason, he never let me sink financially; he always helped me. But emotionally, that was another story. I truly believed that he cared, really, really cared, but he carried a great deal of guilt. I firmly believe that he loved me, and who knows, maybe, in some secret corner of his heart, which he always talked about, in that little corner of his heart that no one can reach – like that little part of one's brain that no one can understand but that carries all the things that you fail to say, the things that you as a person know but don't show, the things we will never repeat, the things that we will carry to the grave, our deepest, deepest darkest secrets and feelings, and I know he has many –in that little corner of his heart I know I will always have a special place.

Everyone remembers 9/11. It will go down as one of the worst days in United States history. I remember that Kamil and I were once up on top of the World Trade Center. He took me there for drinks one night many years ago. It was such a beautiful place; we sat on the top looking out over the incredible city and all its lights of wonder. It was like being on top of the world. The name of the World Trade Center was very appropriate. 9/11 was a very sad day for so many people worldwide. Besides my dearest friends, Jack and Jill, Kamil was the second person I tried to contact that day because I was living in California at the time. I was in a very despondent mood prior to this because I had just lost my dear cousin Rhonda from a freak accident, and I was driving home from Palm Springs that weekend when it happened. I was on my cell phone desperately trying to get through to Kamil, but needless to say, I was unable to. No one could get through that day. Knowing that he had his business in Midtown New York, knowing that New York was in total chaos, I worried for his safety, his children's, and his family's. Two or three days later when I finally got in touch with him, he sounded so sad, sad for the country, sad for what had gone on. Even though this isn't the country of his birth, the U.S. meant a great deal to him. When he learned that his family was okay, he knew he was very fortunate. His children, if they had come into the city that day, would both most likely have died because they both worked on Wall Street. But one was sick, and the other had not gone to work that day. So God was looking out for him and the family he loved. Some people were affected more profoundly than others by 9/11, but all experienced a deep sense of loss and despair.

When I decided to move away from Florida, my first move was to Arizona. A friend of mine had moved there, and she suggested I move there also. It was a spur-of-the-moment decision on my part. I felt it was something I needed to do. Perhaps I was thinking of distancing myself further and further from my Manhattan and Kamil. I just kept running. I had no idea where I was running to; I was just running. I just couldn't get far enough away from everything in my life and my problems. That was in 1998. I went out to Tucson, Arizona. I was there for only four or five months. I procured a job in a woman's dress shop. I hated the location and the job. The scenery was beautiful, but it was not for me. I was not happy there. I had a new apartment, but it was too small. I felt claustrophobic. I felt as if I were going to die. I couldn't breathe in Tucson. After four or five months of living out there, I lost my job. I think I was at the lowest point ever. I had no money, no job. I knew only one person in Tucson. The calmness and warmth of the Arizona desert were not enough to still and comfort my unsettled heart.

To add to my despondency, I received a call one morning from the nursing home in Florida telling me that my mother had passed away, June 21, 1998. In my shock and sorrow, what did I do? I called Kamil immediately to tell him about my mother. Of course, he was very compassionate and consoling. He said how much he loved my mother and said that she was a beautiful woman and that she would be greatly missed. The strangest part of this story is that the following year, I ended up in California working for one of Kamil's best friends, Martin, in a jewelry store, a job, by the way, that saved my life. Kamil had come out to California to attend his friend's wedding, and he had his girl-friend with him, but we did manage to get together. We were all sitting at a table in this restaurant – Kamil, his girlfriend, Martin and his wife, and me. Martin's wife and I were talking about parents, and she was complaining about how difficult her mother was and that she couldn't tolerate her, and I turned around and said, "Don't feel that way because now that my mother is gone, I can truly appreciate what mothers mean. It is comforting to have them in your life – good or bad." I turned around to Kamil and said, "Kamil, tell her how beautiful my mother was." And he looked at me and he looked at her and he said, "What are you talking about? I never knew your mother." At that moment, I thought that everything that I ever felt for him would die. For one instant, for the first time in my life, I hated him because now that my mother had died, he wasn't even acknowledging that she had lived. He acted as if he hadn't even known her; after all these years, he denied her. Lies and denial are a person's downfall. After all those years of caring for her, sending her cards and flowers, making her jewelry, visiting with her and holding her hand when she had her brain hemorrhage, taking her to dinner, sending her presents for Mother's Day, making her promises, and always being there for her – in an instant he denied all of that and her very existence. His girlfriend had gotten up to have a cigarette outside with Martin, and I remember whispering in Kamil's ear, "You son-of-a-bitch." I said to him, "How could you?" He knew exactly what I was talking about. He apologized and said, "I wasn't thinking." I said, "You weren't thinking because you are fucking drunk and went way over the line." I continued to reprimand him, saying, "How could you not remember my mother and say something like that, knowing that she's gone?" I saw a look in his eyes that I will never forget. He said, "Sorry." He looked at me with regret and compassion, but I had none for him. I felt that was the final low blow, and I will never forget that night as long as I live.

But to be fair, there were many good things he did for me. When I was in Arizona, I was so broke that I called him for money. He sent me fifteen hundred dollars. He then told me to call his friend Martin in California and ask him to give me a job in his jewelry store because Martin needed help since his wife didn't want to be in the store that much any more. At first I said, "Don't be ridiculous. I'm not going back to California. That's where I started my adult life." But I had no choice. I was at the bottom of the barrel financially and emotionally. I couldn't even afford to go back to Florida. I called Martin in California, and he told me to come and he would give me a job. I called my cousin in California, Rhonda, who had lived in Beverly Hills with her husband for the last twenty-five years. When I arrived in California, Rhonda picked me up, and I stayed with her. Then I went to see Martin after not seeing him for over twelve years, and that was in New York, with Kamil. Kamil and Martin had come to the United States together as young men. But Martin ended up in California. Most people of his culture settled in Canada, New York, or California. I left Arizona, and I moved to California in a matter of three short weeks, and I immediately started to work for Martin. Of course, I was very thankful to Kamil for recommending me for the job. He started me at fifty thousand dollars a year. Things were working out okay. I had my cousin out there. Martin was an exceptionally good friend and employer.

Strange, here I was back in Sherman Oaks, Studio City, in the Beverly Hills area for the first time since 1963 when I was married to my first husband. I remember that the first couple of weeks I was out there, my cousin and I went to have lunch on Rodeo Drive. Looking across at the Beverly Wilshire Hotel, I said to Rhonda, "Oh, my God, I can't believe that almost thirty years ago I was working at that hotel as a makeup artist." Here I was starting all over again all these years later and all because of Kamil.

Here he was – still a part of my life, still finding me jobs, and still supporting me financially. Back in 1991, when I opened up my own jewelry store in Boca Raton, Florida, Kamil warned me not to open up a jewelry store. But it was something I needed to do, something I had wanted to do my entire life. I wanted my own jewelry store. He said you need two hundred and fifty thousand dollars in the bank to start. I didn't have it. I told him I was going to open it up on a shoestring; again he warned me not to do it. But being the strong-willed person that I am, I did. Of course, he helped me. He gave me all the jewelry, all the mountings that I needed; he sent me invoices just like any other business contact – and I never sent payment. When the store failed and I went bankrupt, he never asked me for a dime. He said, "Forget it!" Was it pay-back time again? Probably! Was that his guilt? Probably! He just looked out for me for whatever reason. I must have owed him at least thirty thousand dollars. He never took a dime. Through the years, anytime he ever gave me money, he never asked for it. Maybe it was because I had given him one hundred thousand dollars to start his business. Perhaps that's the reason. At the time, I had just handed over the money to him without even having him sign a paper. Maybe he felt he owed me all of that. I don't know because it was never discussed; we never talked about it. It was just something he did. Whatever he could do to help me out, he did without question. When I was in Florida and had gone bankrupt, lost my business and my house, and had my mother in assistant living, I needed money. Just before I moved to California, he sent me twenty-five hundred dollars and never asked for it back. I had no credit, so I needed a cosigner to lease a car. I didn't know whom to turn to. It was in 1998, and I called Kamil and asked him to cosign for me. He said, "Just send the papers." He asked no questions. I promised him that I would make the payments on time, which I did. His friend Martin cosigned for my apartment when I moved to California, and I believe that Kamil asked him to do that for me. Kamil was always behind everything when it came to me – assisting me in obtaining a job, helping me financially, getting me a car, buying me anything I needed. He was always there. He was a guy with a huge heart but a heart that never gave to me totally. Was this all motivated by guilt or love? Was I making excuses for him?

To this day, I frequently have strange dreams about him. One dream that confuses me takes place in New York, where I accidentally run into him at a train station. I'm eating alone, and he sees me and then heads to his train. I follow him. He's on the train in a private suite, and he turns, grabs my hand, kisses me, and asks me to stay. I say, "I have my dog, BoBo. How long is the train ride?" He says that he'll take care of it. Then I ask him, "What about your new wife?" He responds, "That is no more." I decide to stay. We get off the train and we go to his apartment. In the apartment, he is talking to his first wife Maria, yet he is with me. It was a weird dream! Was it wishful thinking? Does the dream mean that his marriage is in trouble and I'm his future?

Another recurring dream has me on the streets in New York walking near our old haunt Rockefeller Center, and he is walking toward me with his usual swagger. He looks at me, and I return the gaze, and we realize that after all these years that have passed, our eyes are telling us that everything is the same, which I interpret as meaning that I want it to be that way. I've been haunted by many dreams like these over the years. Only to wake up to the reality that *he* is not with me!

Chapter Twenty Eight

FRIENDS, FINANCES, AND FEARS

This story is also about friendship and about being financially and emotionally dependent on someone who controls your essence and the fear that provokes. Fear of abandonment, loneliness, growing old, and spending the rest of your life without the one you love. Yet, as friends, Kamil never let me down. Was it a form of his love? People say yes. Was he doing it because he had made a promise to my mother that he would take care of me? I'll never know because he is a very private man. He doesn't talk much; it is hard to get into his head. It was impossible to decipher what he was thinking. I know one thing: he always wanted everyone to love him. His children, his wife, his girlfriends, his friends, his business partners – everyone had to love Kamil. He didn't want anyone to say anything bad about him. He tried to be good. He tried to show that he had heart. Yet, in later years that all backfired. He lost a lot of his cherished friends, his adult children that aren't close to him any longer, he divorced his wife Maria, and I'm no longer in his life. All the sacrifices that he made were "For what?" I'm sure he asks himself that question many times over, as I continue to do.

My mother said something to me once, "You come into this world alone, and you go out of this world alone." As I'm getting older, I recognize that is the absolute truth. When everything is said and done, you have only yourself to depend on. I've come to understand that you make your own destiny by making your own choices. You have no one to blame but yourself for whatever you do in your life, including your mistakes. I believe that is what therapy is all about, learning about oneself, learning when to let go, learning to be a good person, learning to be good to yourself, and knowing and admitting one's mistakes. I've experienced and learned a lot in these last twenty years. Some good, some bad: people dying, losing people you love, having good friends who have stayed by you for over thirty years and that remain in your life. My friends are important, especially since I have no husband and no children. I have my dog, my devoted friends, and some scattered relatives here and there, whom I see periodically. That's about it for family; everyone else is gone. I have a half sister, Rene, whom I haven't seen or heard from in years. Basically, I'm alone. As you get older, the only people you have are the friends you can talk to and pour your heart out to. Thankfully, I have wonderful friends, including the writer of this memoir. For her I will always be grateful, especially for her friendship and her love. I have friends who have stood by me throughout all of my mistakes. They never judge me. They give me unconditional love and support. They've stood beside me, they talk to me, they support me, and they where there for me during my unbearable breakup with Kamil and during my deep depression. They were truly concerned about me and, even though we were separated by distance, always contacted me to see how I was. Even during their own personal heartache, they still reached out to me.

When I was living in Arizona, and feeling totally out of control, I called my dear friend Anna and told her that I wanted to end my life because there was nothing to live for. Needless to say, she was extremely concerned. Just to show what a caring and loyal friend she was, she called me every day to check on me. That's a true friend!

I'm a survivor, and that is a critical part of this story. I've survived marriages that failed pitifully, financial disasters, and relationships that didn't work. I've survived not having family and living a lonely existence in New York, Florida, New Jersey, Arizona, and California. I moved seventeen times and left a lot behind, but I was never able to leave behind the memories of Kamil. No matter where I went, they always followed me. He is in my thoughts every day of my life. Who knows what makes somebody care so deeply for another human being? When we're young and we fall in love, it's sometimes for the right reasons and sometimes for the wrong reasons. In my case, it was always for the wrong reasons. My tragic flaw was that I was impressed with the exterior – the surface of a person. I never looked within, especially with both of my husbands. My first husband was clearly a rebound, a person I should never have married. My second husband, David, was a challenge because he was with someone else. I never should have married him either. So what makes someone search for true love and find it? Do we every really know what true love is? Is it fueled by possessiveness? By jealousy? Is it for the want of sex, for the need to feel like we belong, for protection? Are we searching for a father –or mother – figure? Who truly knows? But for some unknown reason, when it is there, you know it. I knew it the first moment I laid eyes on Kamil. I can't describe it. I guess it's that gut feeling. This feeling can last for a period of time or for a lifetime. For me, it was a lifetime. Experts say that love grows slowly between people. At the outset, it is all about attraction and sex; then it matures into mutual respect, consideration, and caring. But I never had that with my husbands. How can you respect someone who doesn't respect you? How can you be considerate of someone who is not considerate of you? Some wives play-act or avoid the reality. They make things look rosier than they really are. I think that is true for many relationships. Perhaps it's because we don't want to confront uncomfortable issues. It seems easier to deny. Most people so fear rejection that they will avoid confrontation at all costs. Love heightens our sensitivities. Any separations, any discrepancies, physical or emotional, wound the partners in love. It is this pain and love that makes us human.

Reflecting back, I see more clearly now that my life with Kamil was never right. We had so many hurdles to overcome. So many other people's lives intertwined with ours: wives, husbands, children, parents, extended families, friends, and colleagues. For some unknown reason, after all these years, I've blocked all that out. He was mine, and that was all that I cared about. Was I giving up a lot? Not really. Was I gaining much? Not really. In retrospect, even though I felt we had a lot, we had nothing; we had no stability, no marriage, no children together, we never shared a home, and no future. We never had many mutual friends. What did we have? What made us click? We were two people from different backgrounds, different religions, different cultures, and an age difference; actually, we had very little in common. Nothing! The only thing we had in common was the jewelry business and our fatal attraction. I was in the business before I worked for Kamil, and he had been in the business since he was ten years old. There is a saying that opposites attract. There was no question that we were opposites. I didn't drink and he did. I didn't do drugs and he casually dabbled. I was a light smoker and so was he. Other than that, what did we have in common? Our incredible sex life? A lot of people are sexually attracted and compatible, but you don't endure a lifetime on casual sex. As we get older, that aspect of a relationship fades. But what never faded for me was that every time he walked into a room, even up to three years ago, he made my heart pound and he made me light up. It's as if he is a permanent part of my heart and soul. I can't let that go.

Professionals and friends say you have to move forward with your life. I did move on by distancing myself from him geographically and getting involved with other men. A whole series of family members died, which made me mature quickly. I changed jobs and careers, and I survived. But what is survival? What does the word *survival* mean? At times, after we separated,

I didn't want to live. You have to be very brave to commit suicide. Fortunately for me, I'm a coward. Did I take drugs? No. I just got through it my own way. I protected myself by putting an impenetrable shield around myself, making it impossible for anyone to get through. I didn't want anyone to get through. Of course, after a while, you get used to it. You get used to living alone and feeling numb inside. You get used to the same mundane routine of going to work, coming home, making dinner, seeing friends, periodically traveling, and after a while, the routine becomes an everyday occurrence. You say that you are happy, but deep down you are not happy because you are missing something. Not because there's no man living in the house – that's not the answer; at least for me it wasn't. I don't need a man living with me. I don't want a relationship with anyone unless I have that wonderful feeling, that excitement of knowing that you want to rush into your house because you know that the person of your dreams is behind that door anxiously waiting for you and he will be lying next to you at night. When the person of your dreams is holding your hand, whether it is walking on the beach or while you are ill – then it's worthwhile. When it is meaningful, then you are fulfilled. Without that feeling, it is just another body living in your house, sleeping in your bed, and sharing your bills. It lacks soul. Of course, even some bad marriages last a lifetime, especially when children are involved. For me, though, I have to *love* the man in my life, and he had to understand me, accept me for who I am, not care if I put on a few pounds and acquire some well-earned wrinkles. He has to look at me when I'm sixty years old and see me as twenty-five. If this doesn't exist in a relationship, then being alone is preferable. I want someone to talk with, relate to, have fun with, sneak a smile at, have a hearty laugh with, and simply enjoy being with – someone who, even if you are not having sex, looks at you adoringly and is content just lying next to you. That is the ultimate romance. That is what most people want from a love relationship. That feeling of caring, wanting to do for the other person, wanting to take care of them, wanting to be there for them, wanting to listen to them – that feeling is wonderful. And even when you disagree or have an argument, you *know* things will be better in the morning. I knew I could have that with Kamil because that is how I felt about him. But it didn't happen. I guess it wasn't meant for us to be together in that type of situation. He always cautioned me that even late in life, we couldn't be together. I think he believed that his friends, his family, and his children would never accept me. Even knowing this, I felt secure because I thought I knew how he felt about me.

A few years after our breakup, Kamil acted as if I didn't exist. He was afraid to talk with me on the phone, afraid to look me in the eye, afraid to have an intimate conversation with me. What was he afraid of? His true feelings? Since he wasn't one to talk about his inner feelings, it was impossible to know why he behaved this way. When things got rough or we had to deal with an issue, he would leave. Days on end, he would not contact anyone – not his wife, not me. I worried sick over him during those times and fearing he was in a hospital or that some ill fate had befallen him or even that he was dead. He would just take off and disappear without a clue. Later I found out that at times he would run off to his shore house, sometimes just drive off somewhere, or even get on a plane. He never even notified his closest confidants, or if they knew, they never told.

Kamil had many secrets, and he hid them well. Many things that went on in his head I was not privy to, even to this day. I do know that for him and me, through all the years that we were together, it was definitely a compassionate love relationship. He proved it to me many times over. He was there to hold my hand in difficult times, he was there when I needed financial assistance, and he was there as my best friend. I told him everything, even after we had broken up. We sat talking on the phone for many hours, discussing everything and anything. Talking, talking, and talking. However, I realize now that I was doing most of the talking. Did he even listen?

It is amazing how a person can control one's mind to make it believe something that doesn't really exist. You make those you love out to be what you want them to be and not actually what they are. I did a lot of that with Kamil. I made him into something he wasn't. I almost made him god-like, which is not healthy. It was as if I didn't want to do anything to make him upset. Did I feel sorry for him? I guess I did. It was if he were a little boy pretending he was strong and had to take care and protect me – when in reality, he was the one who needed to be nurtured and stroked.

It has been a complicated life since 1980 until now, 2004. Reflecting back on this unique relationship with all its convolutions and its changes, it still becomes clear to me that this relationship has become a part of whom I am and where I'm heading. Kamil is married now for the second time to the younger woman who was his customer. Who knows if he is happy? He waited a long time to marry her. Kamil always wanted what his family didn't want him to have. That was part of his rebellious nature. You see, for him, as for me, it was always the challenge that excited us. In the beginning, I was a challenge to Kamil. I was a married woman; I was beautiful and unavailable. He always had an eye for me, and it took him two years to come around when I first met him in 1979. He finally got me. Probably the timing just happened to be right. Who would ever have dreamed that he conquered me for a lifetime – my lifetime. Now I'm in the last quarter of my life. Yes, I am still a vibrant, attractive woman at sixty-four. I still have plenty on the ball. My tragic flaw is that I've pined over one person for over twenty years, and I will most likely die pining over him.

It is amazing how many twists and turns are in this story. As of today, November, 2004, my dearest surrogate family, Jack and Jill, bought an apartment in Florida. This is really amazing because after all these years, my relationship with Jack, his wife Jill, and their two children, who were friends with Kamil, have become my own family. They treat me with respect and love, and they care for me unconditionally. They have become the children I never had, and their children have become my grand-children. It is a wonderful thing that they will be living only a few blocks from me. At Christmas, they always come down here, and I spend it with them. I always wanted to be a mother and a grandmother since I had none of my own, and in my later life that wish has been granted. Isn't it strange? I couldn't have a family with Kamil, but ironically, it was because of Kamil that I met and love dearly my new devoted and beautiful family. Years ago, it was because of Kamil that I met this wonderful, young, shy, caring human being with a heart of gold. I know deep down that even if Kamil were not a part of this, it was destiny that Jack and I would develop our own relationship. Jack was under my wing as a young man starting out in the jewelry business, and now he is "the wind beneath my wing." It wasn't just Jack that took me in; his beautiful wife did also. Jack married an incredible young woman who has an endearing heart. Everyone in her life, children and adults, adore her. No matter what obstacles she faces, she always has a positive attitude. So here I am, a complete outsider, of different backgrounds and faith, and she, like Jack, has embraced me with open arms and heart. To this day, she treats me as she does her own family. She never makes me feel left out. Here is this gorgeous young woman in her forties, a loving wife, a devoted mother, a successful professional, and she calls me her adopted mother-in-law. What more could I ask for in life? Sometimes you don't even have the respect and caring from your own biological children. I'm lucky enough to have it all. I know that if I have any needs, they will be here for me, and for that, I will always be eternally grateful. My mother was right. She always said, "You don't have to be family to have love and respect from another human being because if you are good to the people who are good to you, they become your family whether they are friends, new acquaintances, or just people you meet along the way from all walks of life." I'm living proof of that. And this is where I am at this point of my life, in Florida, in my apartment, working, enjoying my friends, good health, and loving my family – a family that is no blood relationship to me whatsoever. This family proves to me that there is goodness in the world whether you are a blood relative or not. In my personal family, there was nothing but turmoil, hassle, and jealousy, until finally all ties were broken and there was nothing left to salvage. Of course, my parents are gone, and my half-sister, Rene, and I do not speak, and I haven't seen my nieces and great nephews in over ten years. But I am happier than ever because I have my wonderful extended, adoptive family.

Chapter Twenty Nine
SANITY AND SURVIVAL

Most of us live our daily routine of working, eating, sleeping, and for whatever reason, over these last twenty years, I have found a way to maintain my sanity and to survive. At times it was extremely difficult; unbearable. I force myself to push negative thoughts to the recesses of my mind and focus only on beautiful thoughts. You might try to make yourself forget unhappy experiences, but, I believe that deep down, you don't want to forget. I guess that's the way I functioned all those years. Maybe I was searching for some utopia; maybe I was searching for some rainbow at the end of my journey. That never happened. The one thing that did happen over the years was that I learned to live with myself and to be somewhat content and to realize that life isn't all that bad. Many times I was lonely, many times I didn't have a dollar to pay for groceries, but I always held my head high. I believe I got that from my father because he always said, "Never let anyone know what is in your pockets, even if it is your last dime." I believe that was a good lesson for me. On the outside, except for those very close to me who knew the truth, I came across as successful, confident, well-rounded, intelligent, and living the way that someone who has money would live. I never let anyone see that I feared that someday I would be out on the street penniless and homeless. There was a time when I *was* almost out on the street, when I *didn't* know where the next dollar was coming from. My unemployment had run out, and I couldn't ask anyone for money. I sold everything I had – all my jewelry and all the beautiful gifts that Kamil had given me as well as the treasured items my parents had given me. To this day, I have very little left. Remarkably, I got through it all. I have maintained my sanity and believe that I can survive. I know I can survive because I have survived so many things and gotten through so many highs and lows.

Where did this survival mode come from? I believe it's because I was brought up well by parents who indulged me and I thus developed a sense of entitlement. I definitely had a lot of class. I knew how to dress. I knew how to carry myself, and people always looked up to me. I was the girl in school whom all the others wanted to imitate and be like. Truthfully, I wanted to be like them because they had a lot more than I had. Some had the intelligence and wherewithal to pursue higher education; some had great husbands and are still married and have children and close family. Some are financially secure. Some have professional and social power. Some have devoted parents and siblings, and some have loving relationships that have remained secure after many years. And there *I* was – a high school graduate going out with one man after another not knowing where I wanted

to be or where I was going. I never really wanted to study, so I thought college would be a waste of time. I was a free spirit. My dream was to live in Manhattan, go to fashion school, and find that prince in shining armor who would take me away and make my life perfect. My first husband was a very wealthy man from Beverly Hills, so when I married him, I thought *he* was prince and that I gotten the "catch of the century." Was I naïve? Little did I know that he was the complete opposite.

I had poor role models. My mother always lived a lie with my father. She was always conniving and never telling him the truth about why she needed money. Mom spent and gave away so much money that she had to borrow from relatives and banks. She gave money to my sister, her grandchildren, or to me. Did my father know? Probably. She always kept secrets, and that might be the reason why *I* always kept secrets. I can honestly say that no matter what happened in my life, I never felt happy. I never found the happiness that I desired. Not with my family, not with my husbands, and not even totally with Kamil. I thought I was happy with Kamil because during the times we were together, he always thought he gave me what I needed, but that wasn't true. What I needed was to be nurtured by a man who cared about me for *me*, a man who loved me for who I was, a man who wanted to be there for me in sickness and in health and 'til death do us part. Unfortunately, I never had that. I tried. I tried with many different relationships – husbands, lovers, different men who came in and out of my life – until one day I finally realized that none of them gave me what I really needed because I was too afraid to go into a relationship with a full commitment; I always feared being hurt. For me, it was easier to hide behind my wall. This becomes a part of your nature, and with time, it becomes easier and I got used to being alone. I got use to not having a man in my life; I even got use to not craving sex. The reality is that we can fulfill our sexual urges in various other ways, even by finding a person who means nothing. It was easier that way. Seems like, I always took the easy way out. It is easier not to be involved; it is easier to live alone; it was even easier just to work and make a living and not depend on a man.

I had so many talents. I wasted so many years. I should have been very successful. When I did my decorating, I excelled at it but I never went to school for it. When I went into the jewelry business, it was my dream, and even that fell through. I never seem to finish anything. I knew I had the motivation, I knew I had the knowledge, I knew I had the connections, but I never finished anything I started until this book. I will finish this! I will finish this. I will say everything I have to say. I will finish this book because everything else in my life has so many loose ends and this book will tie them all together. As you get older, it gets easier to forget about the loose ends. I was never the type to worry about my future; I lived for the moment. If I had a debt to pay, I determined that I would take care of it – tomorrow. I felt as if my aging would never come. I refuse to concern myself with the fact that I don't have a couple hundred thousands dollars in the bank for my old age. Maybe I do live that adage, "What will be will be." I've always lived on the edge, as my father said.

I never planned for the future even though I am a perfectionist, even though I plan every moment of the week, even though I like to know what I'm doing the following weekend or whatever. When it came to my future, as my father always cautioned me, "Put money aside for the future because before you know it, you'll be senior citizen," but at that time – I was so young and frivolous – I wasn't thinking along those lines, so I didn't prepare. I never saved a dime. I spent every single penny I made even when I was married and even when I wasn't married. Yet I managed to find a way to survive.

I'm a woman with my parents gone and with no assistance from a husband, I have survived. I always made a decent living, and I paid my bills. Ten years ago, I had a bankruptcy, and now I drive a Mercedes. I just seem to survive. I always liked the best things in life. I continue to take a vacation once a year, I go on a cruise, and I manage to buy that designer dress at Saks Fifth Avenue, a designer bag, and costly shoes – but now I look for sales. I always strived and had the best. I might not have as much as I used to but I'm satisfied. When I married my first husband and we lived in Beverly Hills, I had eight closets filled with my things. There wasn't enough room in the apartment for all my clothes, and I continued to buy more and then some more. It seems like I always wanted to own my own things. I never wanted to borrow from anyone. Yet I let people borrow from me. Whatever it was that I owned – homes, furniture, cars, jewelry, clothes – I always wanted them to be the best. Maybe not the most expensive, but always looking the best. I remember making a comment to one of my friends years ago. "I might not have a pot to piss in, but when I put on my mink coat and my boots and walk in Manhattan, boy, do I look like a million dollars." That is the truth. I've been that way my entire life. I always look like a million dollars; it doesn't matter whom I'm with or where I go. And when I reflect back, I think that's a big part of what scared men away from me. They looked at me and thought they couldn't afford me. Little did they know that I really didn't have that much, that it was just a façade.

I recall once when I first moved to Boca and I had a date. The guy came to my door to pick me up; he drove a Cadillac, he was around my age, and he walked into the villa that I had bought, and said, "Boy, you must have a lot of money." Needless to say, it rubbed me the wrong way. I realized at that moment that he was the type of guy looking for a woman who had money that he could live off of; he wasn't the type who wants to take care of anyone or even share the caring. He's the prototype for today's female/male relationships: women pay their own way and men pay their own way. What happened to male chivalry? What happened to all the men who used to pick up the tab for a woman and who would never think of letting a woman pay for anything? The men-take-care-of-women tradition of our parent's generation no longer exists. I think men *caused* women to become stronger and more independent. Women work, we make money, and we pay our own bills. As the years pass, our attitude becomes "If I'm going to pay for myself, who needs them?" This might sound self-centered and selfish, but at least I'm honest. Most of the men in my life have not left me in a secure position. The only position they wanted me in was in the bed. Cynical? Yes. I take some responsibility for my actions that have led me to this point of my life, but in defense, I also gave a lot to the men in my life. Most men I meet today do not want to nurture women. They are too engrossed and involved with their own problems, and they don't want to take on anyone else's. Even with these attitudes, I feel that I have survived. Or did I? Perhaps I hide behind these thoughts and am just trying to convince myself that I don't need a man because he wouldn't support me or would chose not to support me or would want to divide everything down the middle. I equate it to going to bed with someone you love and having two beds instead of one. That is basically what relationships are today. And if you are fortunate enough to find someone who is nurturing and caring, they want a prenuptial agreement. People today do not want to share, and men especially do not want to share their wealth with women, even young couples and anyone entering a first-time marriage. Most couples that come together for the second or third time have children and grandchildren, and they become their priorities. Here is where I become cynical again. Relationships become fragmented. I guess I need total commitment; devotion, caring, support, and I want a person who puts me first in all categories. As we get older, we rethink exclusive relationships. We get concerned about getting ill and having to have someone care for us or about winding up having to care for the other person. It's no surprise that many people think about these things and fear total commitment. A single life *can* be preferable. And if we were to want marriage, sometimes we might not have the opportunity. So feeling good about who you are, being independent, maintaining good friendships, and having stimulating interests can make for a near-perfect life.

In today's society, there are so many demands put on marriage. What happened years ago, when people loved each other, cared about each other, married, and went on to live a life in good times and bad times? Some lasted, some experienced divorce, but in general, they maintained a close family relationship. Most people today aren't even happy with their careers or where they work. I hear over and over again that most workers do not like getting up in the mornings. I speak to many of my friends who are now in their sixties. They claim that they don't have the stamina or the patience any longer to deal with a demanding career. They don't want to work full time, but most of us do not have the option to do otherwise, especially single people. We have to pay high rents or mortgages, car payments, food, and expensive health costs. Most of us *have* to do it, and I'm one of them. Looking back, I can't recall loving a job other than when I worked at the jewelry store with Kamil. I believe that when people feel loved, even their difficult lives are more bearable. Loving Kamil gave me eternal youth and extraordinary stamina.

Chapter Thirty
LIFE'S TRUTHS AND CAUTIONS

What is the truth about life? We are put on this earth, we work hard, bring up families, hopefully, outlive our parents and sometimes, sadly, even our children, relatives and dear friends, and in the end, what do we have to show for it? Not very much! So we go into life naked and we leave life naked. You work fifty or sixty years of your life just to survive. The key to life's truth is to endure life's challenges with dignity and respect for all. For no matter how we live our lives or what we do with our lives, it is all about survival.

I guess you can say that my cynicism comes from my relationship with Kamil. The loss of love, the loss of a life I adored with him, and the loss of the dream of the "Knight in Shining Armour" coming to take me away into a fantasy world. Many of us go through life having unfulfilled dreams and unfulfilled fantasies. However, I lived a life that most people never lived. I experienced a deep and abiding love – one that has lasted a lifetime, and that is one of life's truths. Yes, I experienced great passion and great pain. Would I trade my life? No. Would I have done things differently? Yes!

I hope my cautionary tale of endless uncontrollable passion leads you to make the right decisions in your life. Know full well that the heart dictates our actions when it come to love and that one must be willing to make great sacrifices. Be true to yourself and try to live a life in which you are willing to accept the decisions and actions you made. Remember to look long term and anticipate that your actions will dictate your life. Pain and passion can be rewarding if we view them as life's experiences and if we remain open to forgiving others and ourselves for our past mistakes. If possible, of course, avoid ever making those mistakes.

Love should bring only happiness, we mistakenly think. But love, giving it and receiving it, beckons us to bare our souls, to expose our hidden selves. This is my unique love story; my authentic life story—with its discrepancies and indiscretions. But first and foremost, my life is one of survival and love, a life of enduring friendships, great memories, great joy, and great growth. Now isn't that the real truth about life? My life continues today, and I look forward to the future with great anticipation and expectations.

Epilogue

Since the completion of this memoir, things have changed. Most importantly, I no longer feel the same way about Kamil and, let me make it clear, I do not seek revenge. He has fallen from grace and has been extracted and permanently evicted from my heart. Thank goodness! It began about a year ago, in March. As I had always done, I called Kamil to wish him a Happy Birthday, and when he answered the phone, he was extremely nasty, like a mean drunk. With rage, he shouted at me, "What the hell do you want?" Then he hung up. About a week later, I received a letter from him and the letter read, "I don't want to hear from you any more. I'm happily married." That was basically it. Needless to say, I was extremely upset because over the years we had kept in contact, and I had always called him for his birthday. I wanted to send him a letter, but I knew that when he saw the postmark, he would know it was from me and wouldn't open it. I had to send this letter, so I called my friend in Boston and told her I would be sending her a letter in another envelope and for her to send the inner letter addressed to Kamil and mail it from Boston.

By my sending this letter, I finally put everything to rest. The letter stated that he was self-absorbed, selfish, and inconsiderate.

I felt once again betrayed by this man since he took our friendship with all of its ups and downs and just slammed it shut in my face. In the past he always treated me with respect and kindness. Now he was completely disregarding my feelings and those of everyone from the past who were dear to him. I know for a fact that now, on this day in March 2008, that he turned out to be a man I never expected he would become. My journey with him has finally ended. This is the *"Longest Goodbye!"*

LaVergne, TN USA
19 October 2009
161278LV00002B/63/P